The Art of Business

*It's Alive! The Convergence of
Information, Biology and Business*
WITH CHRISTOPHER MEYER

Lessons from the Future

Future Wealth
WITH CHRISTOPHER MEYER

Blur
WITH CHRISTOPHER MEYER

The Monster Under the Bed
WITH JIM BOTKIN

2020 Vision
WITH BILL DAVIDSON

Future Perfect

Managing Corporate Culture

Managing & Organizing Multinational Corporations

Matrix
WITH PAUL LAWRENCE

Workers & Managers in Latin America
WITH LOUIS WOLF GOODMAN

Comparative Management

Stan Davis **and** *David McIntosh*

The
Art
of
Business

Make All Your Work
a Work of Art

BK

BERRETT–KOEHLER PUBLISHERS, INC.
San Francisco

BERRETT-KOEHLER PUBLISHERS, INC.
235 Montgomery Street, Suite 650 San Francisco, CA 94104-2916
TEL: 415-288-0260 FAX: 415-362-2512 www.bkconnection.com

The poem "Money" by Dana Gioia is reprinted
on pp. 83–84 with the permission of the author.

ORDERING INFORMATION
QUANTITY SALES Special discounts are available on quantity purchases
by corporations, associations, and others. For details, contact the
"Special Sales Department" at the Berrett-Koehler address above.
INDIVIDUAL SALES Berrett-Koehler publications are available through
most bookstores. They can also be ordered directly from Berrett-Koehler:
TEL: 800-929-2929; FAX: 802-864-7626; www.bkconnection.com
ORDERS FOR COLLEGE TEXTBOOK/COURSE ADOPTION USE
Please contact Berrett-Koehler: TEL: 800-929-2929; FAX: 802-864-7626.
ORDERS BY U.S. TRADE BOOKSTORES AND WHOLESALERS
Please contact Publishers Group West, 1700 Fourth Street,
Berkeley, CA 94710. TEL: 510-528-1444; FAX: 510-528-3444.

Library of Congress Cataloging-in-Publication Data
Davis, Stanley M.
The art of business : make all your work a work of art /
Stan Davis and David McIntosh.
p. cm.
Includes bibliographical references and index.
ISBN 1-57675-302-6
1. Creative ability in business. I. McIntosh, David, 1958– II. Title.
HD53.D385 2004
650.1—dc22   2004057395

FIRST EDITION
09 08 07 06 05   10 9 8 7 6 5 4 3 2 1

For Barbara Davis

and for Julius and Margery McIntosh,

who have invested so much

in art and people

CONTENTS

Act Three: See Your Work as a Work of Art

Act Four: See Your Customers as an Audience

Exit Music 183

Whether your business is a factory or a farm, an office or an opera company, there are benefits from bringing an artistic perspective to your work. Many people feel the arts are important in their private lives but don't have a place in their work world. Our book is meant to be a bridge across that divide.

The Art of Business describes a way of looking at business that is as important, productive, and profitable as the more conventional one. Historically, the business world has focused on the *economic flow* of business: first on owning, controlling, and employing the necessary economic inputs; then on carrying out the economic processes in the value chain more efficiently than anyone else; and ultimately on satisfying the customers' desires for economic outputs that are better, faster, cheaper, and safer.

We aren't saying you should stop caring about these traditional economic inputs, processes, and outputs that make up your business. Far from it. Our point is that there are many valid ways of seeing things. It's not an either/or matter; you don't have to choose. It's a duality of "Yes, and . . ." Some people have asked us if the goal of the book is to help people be more successful or achieve greater happiness.

Business books try to do the former, and self-help books the latter. Our answer, again, is both.

We will show that business also has an *artistic flow.* The flow begins with artistic inputs you can draw on, such as the imagination, emotion, intelligence, and experience inside you and your organization. Artistic processes—creating, producing, and connecting—then transform these raw materials into finished work. And downstream, the artistic outputs of these processes satisfy customers' desires for beauty, excitement, enjoyment, and meaning.

When we started work on *The Art of Business*, we knew the difficulty the arts and business have communicating with each other. We both came from business backgrounds and had lifelong interests in the arts. Stan, a business strategist and futurist, was a professor at the Harvard Business School for over a decade, a board member of a management consulting firm, the author of twelve business books, and a frequent speaker at business conferences worldwide. David was an investment banker, management consultant, and executive development specialist. We often found ourselves invited to address arts groups at their board meetings and annual conferences. Eventually we joined some of those boards, including those of the Boston Ballet, Jacob's Pillow Dance Center, and Opera America, the industry association for 197 opera companies around the world. Our role was to bring in outside perspectives from business.

Overture

We've always felt able to communicate equally well with the arts and business. We've observed that business can learn countless things from the arts—such as managing creativity, identifying talent, finding meaning in work, and working toward peak performances. We've seen approaches and attitudes in the arts that can revitalize the organizations where most of us work. We acknowledge those who feel that art should exist only for art's sake, but we feel art can also exist for a host of other reasons, whether economic, psychological, religious, or otherwise. We've brought that perspective to this book.

We have organized *The Art of Business* around the elements of the artistic flow. In the opening section we introduce the ideas of dualities and artistic flow. The next three sections address the main components of the artistic flow: the inputs, processes, and outputs. Each of these contains a pair of chapters—one that lays out the framework, and a second that shows how to put it into action. We end with a coda that gives you more than twenty concrete ideas for bringing the artistic flow into the work you do.

When you see your work as a work of art and your customers as an audience, you'll run your business more profitably. And when you see your work as a work of art and yourself as an artist, you'll find more satisfaction in what you do.

Think of your two eyes as separately representing artistic and economic vision. You can see with either one eye or the other, but you need both to have depth perception. When you see the world simultaneously with an eye for art and an eye for economics, you have much greater depth in business perception.

All of us—business executives and artists, audiences and consumers—benefit from seeing the world with both an aesthetic sensibility and a strategic bent. Integrating the arts and business, bringing together our individual aesthetics and the work we do, managing the economic and the artistic flows of business—that's what we mean by the art of business.

STAN DAVIS AND DAVID McINTOSH

Boston, Massachusetts ~ October 2004

See with Both Eyes

CHAPTER ONE

The Artistic Flow of Business

On stage was a six-foot-square sheet of black paper with about eight buckets of paint on the floor in front. We were in Boston's Museum of Science, after dinner, at a business conference. The artist came out, chatted with the audience for a few minutes about what he was going to do, and then began to paint.

He used his hands as brushes, thrusting and cupping them into various buckets, then flinging, spattering, and smearing the paints onto the canvas. The colors, Day-Glo orange, lively chartreuse, electric blue, and the like, made a vivid contrast with the black sheet. Tony Bennett sang on the sound track. The artist spoke to the audience as he created, telling them that he needed their enthusiasm and involvement for inspiration. The room began to pulsate gently with foot tapping, some encouraging call-outs, and general enjoyment.

Within a couple of minutes you began to see that he was painting a portrait and by coloring the negative spaces, not the hair but the background arc around the hair. Around three songs or fifteen minutes later, he finished with a flourish of splatter for good measure, and there it was—a very alive-looking portrait of Tony Bennett in midsong.

He went on to do Albert Einstein. Then, during his third and final portrait, he played Jimi Hendrix music. By now the crowd was really with him, and the flinging and splashing paint matched the energy of the music and the room.

Soon, however, people began to notice that this one didn't look a lot like Jimi Hendrix. You could imagine his face, but more because you wanted the performance artist to succeed than because Hendrix's likeness was really emerging there on stage.

The artist paused, stepped back, and shook his head. He turned to us and said, "You know, sometimes they just don't turn out." Then he looked back at the canvas for a long moment, cocked his head, walked up to the portrait, turned it 180 degrees around, and there it was—an electrifying, perfect likeness, with paint splatters of sweat flying off Hendrix in concert. We all loved it.

As a coda to the story, we're told the artist would sell the portraits for a four-figure amount. Sometimes they'd be for a charity fundraiser, sometimes they'd be prizes, and sometimes they'd just be for sale. A few years later we saw one behind the couch in an executive's office.

Why even have art at a business conference? To inspire people to think creatively, to see the many ways to look at the blank canvas of a business problem. And was his work art or entertainment? Was this visual art or performance art? You must be kidding, of course, if you think in each case it was one and not the other.

Most people find it difficult to operate with two perspectives simultaneously in mind, couplets like art and business, meaning and success, life and work, self and other, profit and beauty—the list is endless. The trick is to see these as dualities, irreducible and complementary points of view that we need to hold at the same time. When we embrace them this way, we can find contexts large enough to hold both halves. The mark of a first-rate intelligence, F. Scott Fitzgerald said, is the ability to hold two contradictory thoughts simultaneously and still function.[1] We think most everyone can do that.

When scientists look at the world that way, they see light

is both wave and particle, time and space are not separate, and you cannot know position and momentum at the same time. When artists do that, they show comedy can raise tragedy to greater heights, three-dimensional depth can be portrayed on two-dimensional surfaces, and music can express formal elegance and emotional truth at the same time. When businesspeople do that, they prove quality and profit are not opposites, innovation and efficiency are compatible with one another, and producers and consumers can co-create.

Arts and economics can also blend, but generally they don't. Most of us feel both arts and economics are important to us as individuals, but we relegate economics more to our work and the arts more to our personal lives. This doesn't have to be. An artistic sensibility flows through business as much as an economic one does. But it gets much less attention, because the traditional business model doesn't know how to handle it. We believe a richer value proposition exists: artistic sensibility improves business performance.

Economic and Artistic Flows

Economic flow is rooted in science and technology and based on the straightforward notion that a business uses resources to fulfill desires. It presumes that people want their products and services to be better, faster, cheaper, and safer. It's a good model, but it ignores other desires. People also want their products and services to bring meaning, beauty, enjoyment, and excitement to their lives. These desires are addressed by the artistic flow.

Both economic and artistic flows have a direction and an inevitability to them, like water flowing downhill: things go in one direction, from raw materials to satisfied customers. The two flows have the same elements of *inputs* transformed by *processes* into *outputs.* The two flows are different because of how they define these terms.

Inputs. In the economic flow, the resources are called raw materials or factors of production—specifically land, labor, and capital. The artistic flow of a business, on the other hand, starts with a different set of resources. Artists' resources go beyond tubes of paint and sequences of dance steps. The most important resources in the artistic flow are imagination, emotion, intelligence, and experience.

Processes. At the heart of both flows are the processes they use to transform inputs into outputs. In business, the total set of a business's processes is called its value chain. The steps in a value chain typically include research and development, manufacturing, distribution, sales, marketing, and overhead functions—or simply, create, produce, consume. These processes are also at work in the artistic flow: magic happens when artists create, performers perform, and audiences appreciate.

Outputs. Both business and art succeed when they know the people they address and the markets they serve. Businesses thrive when they meet customers' desires that were waiting to be discovered. Who imagined that instant messaging was going to be the "killer application" for online teenagers, the software that made the hardware worth having? Who would have thought people would want famous opera themes as ring tones on their cell phones? In the artistic flow, many desires are at work. Creators and consumers need beauty, excitement, enjoyment, and meaning. Not only do people look for these in art, they look for them in their lives. Economic needs are more basic, but not more important, than artistic needs.

British novelist C. P. Snow described two cultures—science and humanities—each aware of the other but speaking such different languages that one couldn't see value in what the other was doing.[2] So it seems with the economic world and the artistic world. *The Art of Business* has a more modest goal than Snow's, not to heal a breach but to show how business can benefit from an artistic perspective. The two models of economic flow and artistic flow don't require choosing one or the other. They are complementary, not contrary.

Why Now?

Five decades ago, the Industrial Age reached its high water mark and the Information Age began. Today the Information Age has matured, and three basic forces are now propelling us to pay attention to the artistic flow in business.

First, *sound and images* will become as important as numbers and text for the way business is conducted.

Second, sound and images carry *emotionally richer communication* than numbers and text.

And third, customers are embracing these changes faster than employees; they are happening *faster outside than inside* the organization.

Business is not prepared for these shifts. Creative artists and the consuming public have embraced digitalized sound and images, while managers and administrators have not. Business needs to pay attention now to the artistic flow, not because it's a nice thing to do, but because technological and market conditions are leading it there and will demand it.

Sound and Images. In today's economy, information comes in four forms: numbers, text, sound, and images. Information, of course, also comes in many other forms—such as intuition, emotions, smell, taste, and touch—but we do not yet have technologies to manipulate how we create and communicate them the way we do for numbers, text, sound, and images.

The first killer applications of the information economy were number-crunching programs for payroll and book-keeping. Two decades later came word processing and, after that, the spreadsheet. Not until the 1990s did digital become the preferred format for sound (speech and music) and images (photos, graphics, and videos). Then presentation software like PowerPoint became another new killer app.

Numbers and text are still the workhorses for conveying information in science, technology, and business. Sound and images, by contrast, are more common in arts and entertainment, performance, and social expression. Now this is changing, due to faster, cheaper computers, data compression formats and algorithms, and broadband internet. More tools are in the toolkit. Mundane administrative tasks are enriched with more emotive and aesthetic information. Short and simple e-mails, for example, routinely link to visually rich websites. In the future, effective leadership and connections to customers will rely more on sound and images than just on plain words.

Emotionally Richer Communication. Routine phenomena of business administration are still handled overwhelmingly by numbers and text. A few specialized business activities, though, like product design, branding, advertising, and corporate identity, have long relied on sound and image.

As the vehicles we use for communicating evolve, so does the amount of emotional content we invest in those communications. The abundance of digital computing and communicating power is making emotionally and aesthetically rich information flows a more frequent part of daily business life. The richer the communication, the more emotion we share.

E-mail is a text-based killer app, for example, but see (or rather read) how it is morphing. E-mail is slowly becoming more emotionally and aesthetically rich, as it becomes easier to make pictures and sounds part of the message. Instant messaging, the next major generation of e-mail, is a much more human and emotional form of exchange than its predecessor.

Digital cameras are helping bring the same shift now that they've reached critical mass and replaced film cameras in most households. What's the first thing you do with a digital camera after you take a picture of someone? Look at it, show it to them, and talk about it.

In fact, Stan routinely carries a digital camera in his pocket that literally fits into an Altoids box. Its postage-size chips, inserted into a machine at our neighborhood Walgreens, will burn a CD of 150 high-quality photos, for a few dollars, while we wait. In a reverse flow, it won't be long before feature movies will migrate off CDs and DVDs into the same tiny boxes that we carry in our pockets.

Cell phones, since they can communicate both information and emotion, are becoming the most important piece of technology for most people. Cell phones (sound) are absorbing e-mail functions like messaging and PDA functions like calendars (text), rather than the other way around. They are also taking pictures (images). The applications are migrating to the devices that hold the greatest "emotional bandwidth."

Web logs are another increasingly popular case of rich self-expression. These "blogs" are web-based personal diaries, stream-of-consciousness jottings, and essaylike reflections, posted as soon as their authors write them. The best ones develop followings of readers and fans, while others have a more limited circulation. Today's blogs are mainly text-based, though emotionally rich; they'll increasingly broaden to sound and images. If Andy Warhol were still alive, he would say that, in the future, everybody will be famous for fifteen readers.

With each new generation of both hardware and software, human connections are richer and more immediate. Digital applications become more and more tuned to human connections, qualities, emotions, and even economics. We are moving from communicating economic information in cut and dried forms to communicating in ways that are by their nature more aesthetically and emotionally rich. The arts have as much (or more) to say about these things as does economics.

Faster Outside Than Inside. Changes in technology and communications are being adopted and exploited faster among consumers than in the workplace. Consumers have aesthetically richer information lives than employees, even when the same people switch roles between home and office.

If you see a manager using his laptop on an airplane, look at the screen. If he has numbers or text on it, he's probably working; if he has sound or images operating, he's probably relaxing. This isn't because the different forms are suited to different activities. It's because companies are slower adopters than are customers. Too many managers still think that PowerPoint slides are the frontier for visually rich corporate communication. They ought to look up from their laptops more often.

A hundred years ago, the high-tech way for business to communicate was by telegraph. The ability to communicate with dots and dashes transformed financial markets, transportation systems, and even warfare. The telegraph was such a successful technology that when the next new thing—the telephone—came along, Western Union took a pass. They couldn't imagine how it could be a significant improvement over what already existed. In hindsight, the ability to communicate voices and not just data over the wire transformed business once again. If Western Union had paid attention to artistic elements like meaning and emotion (telegrams, after all, told people about births, marriages, and deaths), they would have rethought what economic elements like faster and cheaper meant.

The business world today is showing a similar lag in embracing the new technologies. Music and entertainment industries are leading the way, but ironically the customers are doing the embracing, not the executives. The "suits" are resisting the change tooth and nail, litigating and intimidating their customers. Unfortunately for them, a business that alienates its customers isn't destined to survive. If they can't create new business models that embrace these technologies, how can they possibly embrace the same technologies to advance their administrative practices and managerial mindsets?

The work world will eventually catch up as today's teenagers and twentysomethings become tomorrow's managers. As they move into and up the work hierarchy, their habits will draw on software that relies ever more heavily on sound and images. Their communication will have greater richness and density of information, more juice and affect than a smiley face emoticon. It would be a pity to wait for another generation to fill the managerial ranks before this happens.

The Artistic Flow of Business

If you want further evidence of where change is happening, look for the verbs. Very successful applications (nouns) get used as verbs when they become part of our behavior. Want to improve the photo you just took, why not "photoshop it"? Search engines like Google went from being oddities to mainstream in five years. Now, if you want to know about someone, want the answer to a question, or want to research a topic, you just "google it." Soon, if you want to know where something is, you'll "GPS it." When popular applications shift from nouns to verbs, it's a sure sign that they've made it into our everyday actions; they've become the common and normal way to do things. They've migrated from everyday tools to everyday conduct.

These three changes taken together—the importance of sound and images, emotionally rich communications, and their adoption faster outside than inside corporations—will require businesses to change their ways of doing things. The artistic flow is now as important in business as the economic flow, and the real benefits come from weaving the two together. Companies that incorporate artistic elements into their economic flow will have a distinct competitive advantage over competitors holding on to today's version of the telegraph.

Déjà Vu All Over Again

We realize this whole notion of blending artistic and economic flow may seem unfamiliar. When new ideas come into the work world, it takes a while before they become conventional wisdom. Around two decades ago, for example, the business world paid no attention to the notion of culture. Then a few business writers and consultants picked up on the idea that, like countries, all companies have cultures that bear significantly on performance and the way things get done. Stan, for example, wrote a book on the subject (*Managing Corporate Culture*) and was featured in *Fortune* and *BusinessWeek* cover stories, the latter depicting corporate culture with Easter Island statues dressed in business suits.

Many companies said, "Yes, we've got a strong culture" and trumpeted the specifics. Others said they didn't know how to define it, but they were sure it existed in their companies. Consultants often helped them spell out what it was, what they wanted it to be, and the steps needed to close that gap. Today, the notion of "corporate culture" has survived the consultants and the gurus. It is a standard term in the business vocabulary, an accepted and honored concept, not a buzzword that disappeared as quickly as it sprang up.

We believe that artistic flow is another such concept.

The Artistic Flow of Business

Corporate cultures are about the unwritten rules, the way things get done inside; artistic flow is about bringing aesthetic and emotional dimensions into all your work and business. This means bringing artistic flow into your products and services, to your customers and markets, to the ways you create, produce, and consume, and into the ways you manage and administer your organization. Not because it's pretty but because it's smart. Today, the business world says, "Huh, what does this have to do with us?" In the future the importance of artistic flow will simply be assumed. It will be a basic business term, another fundamental perspective.

Seeing in a New Way

The Art of Business is about seeing both the economic flow and the artistic flow in business. Enormous benefits result from applying and blending insights from two worlds—the aesthetic and emotional richness of the arts and the strategic and operational perspective of business. You can see textures where everybody else is seeing shapes. You can see colors where others see grays. You can see not just what is, but what could be.

In business strategy, the four cardinal elements are always you, your offer, your customers, and your competitors. If you've got a clear, differentiated view about how those four pieces fit together, you've got a strategy. But now, if you are managing both the economic flow and the artistic flow of your business, you will slightly change how you see these four elements.

See yourself as an artist. You don't need to be a Dilbert-esque drone, trapped in a cubicle farm. Work can be ennobling. You can create things—new products or services, new experiences for people, or even a new atmosphere for getting things done. In any of these cases, you are creating something meaningful that wouldn't have existed if you hadn't been there. There's an aesthetic to that.

See your work as a work of art. Work doesn't need to be about what you do; make it about what you create. Punching a time clock isn't creating something, but making a customer happy is. Going to meetings might not be creative, but building a strong organization is. A work of art shows a human's touch. It's designed to be appreciated by someone else. It has some lasting value.

See your customers as an audience. If you see yourself as an artist and the work you do as art, then your audience will be a full partner in your enterprise. They will feed you as much as you feed them. You co-create. Nominally, you give them your offer, and they give you their money. If there are aesthetics in your strategy, if there is beauty in your offer, if there is elegance in your exchange—then they will also give you their emotional involvement. This is a far cry from the way most businesses deal with work, where two people are trying to get the better of each other before they walk away. Audiences and customers are part of the creative process. You can't create art without an audience; you can't get emotional commitment from customers without an aesthetic in your exchange.

See your competitors as teachers. Throughout their long careers, Picasso and Matisse saw each other as rivals rather than friends. But they followed each other's work intimately. Matisse once wrote to Picasso, "We must talk to each other as much as we can. When one of us dies, there will be some things the other will never be able to talk of with anyone else." You can learn as much from your competitors as Picasso and Matisse did. You and your competitors are going after the same audience, but you are equipped with different strengths and have different perceptions of what the audience will respond to. Studying your competitors, you can learn what they are doing that you would never want to, and you can establish what you are able to do that they can't. By studying them, you can learn about yourself.

We can imagine some people pushing back and saying, "But I'm not an artist." Wrong. Being an artist is like being a tennis player. You don't have to play every minute of the day, but you do it often enough to describe yourself as a tennis player. And if you are occasionally creative, if you deliver a beautiful serve or drop shot, if once in a while you do things that other people can appreciate, you are already a sometimes artist. That's enough to get started and to make it worthwhile.

What Life Could Be Like

"The purpose of art is to lay bare the questions which have been hidden by the answers," wrote novelist James Baldwin. In business, we are too often so sure we know what customers want that we stop questioning ourselves. During the last several decades, most of us focused on satisfying our customers' needs for better, faster, and cheaper goods and services. Doing that, we lost sight of deeper needs and ways to make our lives more enjoyable, more beautiful, more balanced, more meaningful.

One of our favorite cartoons, clipped out and saved over twenty years ago, is captioned "Life Without Mozart." It's a drawing by Mick Stevens of a desolate, despoiled landscape. An empty bottle, a flat tire, a few other pieces of trash, and nothing beautiful—or even interesting—as far as the eye can see. That's what life is like with the beauty and meaning stripped away. That's what life is like without artistic flow.

Now, instead of thinking what life without Mozart would be like, ask what life—or work, or even art—would be like if it had more beauty and meaning; if our reports had images and sound to accompany the text; if our office windows looked out on the water instead of the back of another office building; if our neighbors told us how much our products add to their lives. Life would be a lot more terrific, more fulfilling. Our work would be better, and we'd get better results out of it. This is what comes from understanding and managing the artistic flow of business.

CHAPTER TWO

Dualities

"Do you walk to school, or do you carry your lunch?" "Is it colder in the winter or in the mountains?" These are dualities, not dichotomies. Not so much "either/or" as "Yes, and . . ."

A true dichotomy is an either/or thing. Dead or alive. Black or white. But if you take a closer look, a seeming dichotomy often reveals a gray area between the two extremes. There's a difference, for example, between young and old, but there's generally no single birthday when a person goes from being young to being old. The categories of young and old blur into one another, sometimes gracefully, sometimes not.

Would-be dichotomies can also trip people up when they pair two ideas that seem at odds but are actually independent of one another. High quality and low cost, for instance, aren't opposites; something can be one, or the other, or both. Francis Ford Coppola's *Godfather* trilogy was successful as both film and movie, both art and enter-

tainment, both cinematic triumph and box-office block-buster.

In most cases, we are better off seeing the duality obscured by the dichotomy. A duality is a pair of ideas that seem mutually exclusive but aren't. Military intelligence. Mass customization. Aesthetic strategy.

"The opposite of a correct statement is a false statement," said Niels Bohr. "The opposite of a profound truth may well be another profound truth." In other words, a duality.

Recognizing a duality requires us to identify qualities we generally don't look for—that "other" we pay little attention to and the stuff we dismiss as meaningless, irrelevant, or contradictory. Sherlock Holmes solved one of his most famous mysteries by noticing the dog that *didn't* bark.

Drawing from two worlds simultaneously, we can deepen our sense of perspective, like the doctor who works for Médecins Sans Frontières (Doctors Without Borders) and the sales manager who coaches Little League. The same thing happens when a market researcher uses mathematically based science to underpin the artistic direction of a successful ad campaign.

At first blush, "aesthetic strategy" seems to comprise two ideas that don't belong together. Aesthetic means artsy, and strategy means business, or so it might seem. But when we look at them separately and more closely, they come into focus as two views of the same reality.

Aesthetic Richness

Everything has an aesthetic. Or, more correctly, everything can have an aesthetic if you choose to give it one. We're accustomed to sensing an aesthetic when painters capture landscapes, musicians play harmonies, and actors create memorable characters. We're less used to sensing an aesthetic when dentists fill cavities, assembly lines run perfectly, and salespeople satisfy customers. It's there to be seen in routine and useful activities, even if you have to stop and look for it.

When we talk about the aesthetic in a piece of art, we are talking about what the creator wants the audience to experience and appreciate. The music in *West Side Story* has an aesthetic that is jazzy, rhythmic, and operatically lyrical. Leonard Bernstein used a pulsating, angular style to convey the energy and anxiety of teenagers out on tough streets, and long, arching, and lyrical lines to communicate love and grief. The work is more than just its aesthetic, but its aesthetic is what the audience remembers.

We all have aesthetic sensibilities. If you sprinkled parsley on top of a dish, lit a dinner candle, and turned on music to enhance your mood, then you expressed your aesthetic self. Teenagers' bedrooms, with posters taped to the ceiling and dirty laundry on the floor, reveal their aesthetics more than their parents'. One person might look like he slept in a new suit only minutes after first putting it on, while another can sleep on the red-eye and still look stylish.

Our hobbies also reflect our aesthetics. Some people do needlepoint. Some people are gardeners. Some collect guns, or license plates, or almost anything. Whatever our hobbies, the more we learn about them, the more attuned we become to nuances and particulars, to shading and tone. We bring our artistic sensibilities out of the attic. Even if we're not creating high art, to the degree that we're conscious of subtle preferences, we're using our artistic self.

Our cubicles and offices do the same. One of our friends is a psychiatrist. His home office has wine leather chairs, dark wooden bookshelves filled with nonfiction and fiction, readings for work and play, and everywhere are pictures and "tchotchkes," little items he picked up at moments in his life that he wants to remember. He contrasts his workplace with many of his colleagues' aesthetically sterile offices. Since he spends eight hours a day sitting in his office, he wants to enjoy the space. Moreover, he feels that an office with some aesthetic richness helps his clients feel better, more trusting and relaxed.

Every corporate workspace also makes an aesthetic statement. The statement may be "I don't care" or "I care very much," "I like modern" or "I'm traditional," "My office is my space and reflects me" or "Offices reflect the corporate culture." Some scream, "My real life is in the photos, not in the job," and some shout, "The Company, the Company, the Company."

Usually, a common thread runs between different employees at a single office, and you rarely find a random mix of workspace aesthetics. There's engineer gray, there's homey and comfy, there's "We don't fool around" or "We're top of the line (and charge accordingly)," and so on. You can walk into most companies and get an immediate feel for the corporate aesthetic, for the degree to which any one office varies from it, and for what the companies are saying about themselves.

Virtually every aspect of our lives includes an aesthetic component: how we dress, set a table, write a memo, throw a party, decorate a home or office, design or advertise a product. Our ordinary, everyday artistic sensibility says as much about us as do our formal skills, our PowerPoint presentations, and our resumes. When it comes to who we are, the art of the matter gives a richer description than the facts of the matter.

Strategic Perspective

Strategy begins with the very reason your business exists, whether it's to bring beauty into the world, to cure cancer, or to provide healthy food at the lowest cost. Each goal has its own aesthetic.

By contrast, here's something that is not strategy: making a profit. Profit is like health: you can't live without it, but it shouldn't be the reason for your existence. It can tell you how well you're doing, but it can't tell what you ought to do. That's what strategy is for.

Strategy is what the first President Bush called "the vision thing." Lots of people get "vision" and "mission" mixed up, but it's really quite simple. Christ, for example, had a vision and sent out a bunch of missionaries; he didn't have a mission and send out a bunch of visionaries. Bringing forth a creative vision isn't a democratic process; it's a top-down affair for the leader. Visions and missions have different aesthetics.

A strategy is a plan for the ongoing success of your undertaking. Strategies are for the long run. Tactics, not strategy, change to meet circumstances. Strategy is more about policy than operations. Strategy equals a vision plus a plan for action.

A strategy tells people how to act and how not to act. Every decision made, step taken, and performance given is an enactment of the strategy. Is what you are doing today furthering the strategy? If not, fine-tune your actions until you can answer yes. Otherwise, you're wasting time, energy, creativity, and money.

Act One: See with Both Eyes

Strategies have to be clear and memorable. Coca-Cola has been guided for decades by the strategy "within an arm's length of desire." Soda is an impulse purchase, and you have to satisfy impulses immediately or they dissipate. For Coca-Cola this translated into building a ubiquitous distribution system that made Cokes available everywhere.

If the essence of your strategy has to be written down to be remembered, you're not at its core, its central truth. Life is complex, but the truth is simple. This means a strategy should be stated in a simple and distinctive way, one that is repeatable by different people in their own words yet conveys the same essential message. Aesthetic clarity will go a long way to help everyone in a company implement the strategy.

Some time ago we met with the executive committee of one of the largest banks in the country, one that employed around 80,000 people. We had been shown the corporate strategic plan, which read like pretty standard fare. Who else had seen it? "Only those of us in this room and a few planning staff." We asked, "Would the counterpart people in your three main competitors know the basic shape of what you say?" "Sure, as we know theirs," said the chairman. "So," we asked, "whom are you keeping it a secret from? The other 79,975 employees and all your customers?" Outcome: they went public with a Values and Strategy Campaign.

Contrary to popular opinion, your strategy is worthless unless everybody knows what it is. Leaders often keep their strategies secret out of embarrassment or a failure to even have one. A strategy that you're unwilling to share is probably one that's not so hot to look at.

So what does it take to combine aesthetic sensibility and business?

Aesthetic Strategy

An aesthetic is the style, structure, and flavor of a work as experienced by the consumer. Retailers like Ralph Lauren and the Gap have carefully constructed aesthetics—the tastes of the secure rich and of universal youth, respectively, purveyed to the middle class. Southwest Airlines, Ryanair, and JetBlue share an aesthetic that is both economic and artistic: flying can be cheap and fun. The New York City Ballet's aesthetic is to preserve the Balanchine look and feel. IBM's aesthetic is the customer's experience of working with a first-rate vendor who has an unimpeachable reputation and is more than occasionally cutting-edge.

Dunkin' Donuts and Krispy Kreme both have the aesthetic of freshness (not to mention alliterative names). Dunkin' Donuts throws out every pot of coffee after thirty minutes if it's not sold. Krispy Kreme sells the experience of buying donuts right out of the glazing machine while the neon sign in the window flashes "Hot Doughnuts Now."

Not only can a business have an aesthetic, its strategy can have an aesthetic. An artful strategy connects a firm's vision to its capabilities. Even if everyone outside the firm knows the strategy, they probably can't duplicate the web of capabilities that the firm, its suppliers, and its distributors have built up. Everybody knows that Wal-Mart's strategy is "everyday low prices," but that doesn't mean everybody knows the secret to matching their cost structure. Although you may not think Wal-Mart is aesthetic, there's art in a strategy everybody knows but nobody can imitate.

Apple's moves in the recorded music industry are another example of a beautiful strategy. Here's the story. Simple online file-sharing programs sent tens of millions of listeners to other fans, instead of to music stores, to get the tunes they want for free. The music industry—*oligopoly* might be the better word—responded with legal actions against twelve-year-olds and their families in the vain hope that would stop the practice. But you can't alienate sixty million customers; it's simply not a beautiful strategy. CD sales dropped by 30 percent, and the industry still hasn't turned a strategic corner. It still hasn't figured out a viable new business model.

Enter Steve Jobs and Apple. They leveraged their well-known capabilities in user-focused design, and Jobs's clout as CEO of Pixar Studios, to breathe new life into Apple's twenty-year-old strategy of selling integrated hardware and software, instead of one or the other.

Apple's strategy offered music lovers what they want—a legal and easy-to-use interface. Customers could buy songs one at a time for ninety-nine cents each instead of buying them bundled up in albums of uneven quality. First, Apple proved the model worked on their own proprietary hardware, and then they rolled it out on PCs.

Critics said you couldn't take on Microsoft and its Windows Media Player platform; the customers said otherwise. Apple knew that their customers' needs, their competitors' failure to act, and their own capabilities all pointed to the opportunity to do something both "insanely great" and beautiful. Apple is justly famous for its stylish products and its spare, compelling advertising, but its business model for iTunes was one of its most beautiful creations.

Physicists have an expression for this kind of solution. They say that when such elegance and simplicity are in the formulation, you're more likely to be right. Similarly, in detective fiction, an elegant solution is both simple and inevitable. "Elementary, my dear Watson." Aesthetic strategies are elegant—simultaneously simple, stylish, classic, and apt.

Getting to Yes . . . And

As in the case of "aesthetic strategy," getting past the either/or of a false dichotomy is liberating and energizing. We can draw from two pools of resources instead of one, and we can benefit from the experience of successful companies' approaches. At the same time, we can draw on an artistic sensibility that puts us in better touch with our customers' needs and our own capabilities. No either/or choice required. "Do I contradict myself?" asked Walt Whitman. "Very well then I contradict myself (I am large, I contain multitudes.)"

In their classic book *Getting to Yes*, Roger Fisher and William Ury wrote that negotiations don't have to be a game of "I win/you lose."[1] Even though "my interests" and "your interests" might seem like a dichotomy, they're not. When the two sides in a negotiation focus on their interests instead of their bargaining positions, they are much more likely to get to a win-win solution. The greater the differences in what each party is looking for, the greater the opportunity for beneficial outcomes. Or, to put it as a mathematician would, bad negotiations are zero-sum games, and good negotiations are positive-sum. In bad negotiations, one side's demands are met with either a flat-out "no" or, more encouragingly, with a "No, but . . ." In good negotiations, one side's proposal is met by the more promising response "*Yes*, but . . ."

Actors and improvisational comics take "getting to yes" a step further. Sketch comedy like *Saturday Night Live* and improv like *Whose Line Is It Anyway?* operate with one cardinal rule: don't stop the momentum. Wherever the scene finds itself heading, that's where you have to go. You can add to what's going on, but you can't pretend that what has been said and done didn't happen. Actors prepare for group improvisation by doing an exercise called "Yes, and . . ." They tell a story, adding a line at a time to what the person before them said. No matter what convoluted concoction they get handed ("There's this deli and the guy behind the counter is a samurai . . ."), the only response is "Yes, and . . ."

Getting to "Yes, and . . ." is finding the duality in a situation. In this chapter we used the oxymoron of aesthetic strategy as an example of a duality. The strategy side of the duality draws on the economic flow of business: how to commit your resources to satisfy your customers and outmaneuver your competitors. The aesthetic side draws on the artistic flow of business: finding creative ways to meet your audience's subjective needs and to learn from your competitors. The two flows are complementary sides of one duality.

Act One: See with Both Eyes

In the next chapter, we'll talk about the two flows in more detail. We'll talk about the resources that each draws on, the processes they exploit, and the desires they satisfy. Since most people have a greater familiarity with the economic flow of business, we'll spend more time on the artistic flow. But our objective will be to show how the two flows make up a duality. When you start seeing them that way, you'll end up with more resources to work with and better ways of approaching your work. If you can draw on both sides of the duality, you've got a distinct competitive advantage.

CHAPTER THREE

The Elements of Artistic Flow

In Stephen Sondheim's song "Anyone Can Whistle," the singer wonders why she can do difficult things like tango and read Greek but can't whistle, why "what's hard is simple, what's natural comes hard." Like the tango and Greek, economics is hard, but after years in business the economic flow seems relatively clear and simple to most of us. Artistic flow, on the other hand, even though it includes natural things like emotions, imagination, beauty, and meaning, comes hard to people in the business world.

Moving from inputs to outputs is not the only type of flow. Psychologist Mihaly Csikszentmihalyi described *flow* as "a sense of exhilaration, a deep sense of enjoyment that is long cherished and that becomes a landmark in memory for what life should be like."[1] We are engaged, confronting challenges we have the resources to meet, fulfilling our desires, mastering our own fate. A basketball player is "in the zone" when he is playing at the top of his game and everything he does has a kind of magic. Flow is the sense we get when doing something hard feels simple, when we feel in control of our actions.

Likewise, good companies can experience this state of well-being. These are the companies that are better at drawing on both artistic and economic elements. For most companies and most people, this is not easy. They're not used to seeing the artistic resources, desires, and processes around them. They either overlook artistic elements or undervalue what they see.

Our point in this chapter is to give you a framework for the elements of economic and artistic flow—the inputs, outputs, and processes familiar to both worlds. We'll see that they are already familiar to us, and that it's not such a big step to use them more consciously. Then, what had seemed hard—artistic sensibility improving economic performance—will become simple, and what's natural won't seem so hard.

Artistic Inputs in Business

Land, labor, and capital are the classical factors of production, the inputs or resources of any economic flow. Make good use of them, and they can give you a comparative

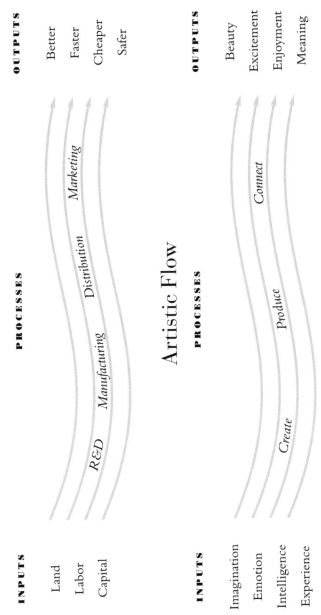

Economic Flow

INPUTS

Land
Labor
Capital

PROCESSES

R&D
Manufacturing
Distribution
Marketing

OUTPUTS

Better
Faster
Cheaper
Safer

Artistic Flow

INPUTS

Imagination
Emotion
Intelligence
Experience

PROCESSES

Create
Produce
Connect

OUTPUTS

Beauty
Excitement
Enjoyment
Meaning

advantage over other firms working with them. But when everyone is working with those same inputs, the differences are likely to be small and short-lived. Add a different variety of resources to the flow, however, and the comparative advantage can be large and long-lasting. Artistic inputs, of course, are a definite source for that variety. When economic orthodoxy requires us to see artistic inputs only as variations on different kinds of labor, it narrows our understanding of the breadth of resources actually available to us.

Imagination is an artistic resource that can transform the dreary economic resource of labor into something more positive. While dreamers and small children have lots of imagination, managers generally show considerably less. Even though the arts treat imagination as fundamental, it seems out of place in the economic model. Business surely recognizes the benefits of imagination but doesn't know how to treat it so that it naturally contributes. Imagination *is* natural, but it comes hard to business.

It doesn't have to be that way. When Julie Taymor was invited to create the staged version of Disney's *The Lion King*, she faced a daunting challenge: to be simultaneously magical and commercial. How do you take cute cartoon characters and have them seem believable on stage? How do you keep it from looking like a sorry version of *Disney on Ice*? Taymor's imaginative leap was to create exquisitely fantastical puppets twice the size of people, magical yet plausible lions and giraffes, meerkats and warthogs. Pixar Studios created similar commercial magic for Disney with its advanced animation technology in films. Too bad, then, that CEO Michael Eisner couldn't bring such imaginative genius to Disney's total business flow. Instead, by the late nineties, stockholders, customers, and employees alike screamed that he was killing the magic—Disney's most important resource and value creator.

Emotion is another resource we all have, but we associate it more with artists than with executives. Artists are keenly aware of emotions, both their own and the ones they're eliciting. By contrast, when businesspeople talk about trusting their emotions, they feel compelled to dress them up in tough-guy talk. Jack Welch's book, after all, was called *Jack: Straight from the Gut*, not *I Feel Your Pain*. Emotions are powerful resources when we can make use of them, but doing so is difficult as long as emotions are associated with words like *soft* and *weak*. Schwarzenegger the politician uses emotions as effectively as Schwarzenegger the action movie star.

The most effective leaders are able to blend the rational and the emotional. Psychologist and journalist Daniel Goleman describes them as having the skill of "primal leadership."[2] When people in an organization see the folks at the top being emotionally grounded, they are more likely to make use of their own emotional resources. The companies that show up in *Fortune*'s Most Admired Companies list are ones where it's okay to show passion, courage, loyalty, and hope. People are proud to work at a company like Johnson & Johnson, and their emotions have as much impact as a firm's economic assets on its bottom line.

Intelligence is another very human resource. Howard Gardner, a psychology professor at Harvard's Graduate School of Education, showed that a lot more smarts exist than just book smarts. He coined the term *multiple intelligences* to describe the broad range of abilities that go beyond the verbal and mathematical intelligence measured on IQ and SAT tests.[3] Although he focused mainly on the implications of these multiple intelligences for new approaches in education, they are tremendously applicable in business.

Artists rely on musical, spatial, and kinesthetic intelligences. The two emotional intelligences Gardner identified as critical for success—interpersonal and intrapersonal—are as closely aligned with an artistic sensibility as with an economic one. *Inter*personal intelligence includes abilities like leading, nurturing relationships, keeping friends, and resolving conflicts. Gifted leaders know how to work with people. They instinctively know when somebody is starting to get upset. *Intra*personal intelligence is the ability to know what's going on with other people and to know what's going on in yourself.

Experience from one domain that can be applied elsewhere is yet another resource. Craig Venter significantly sped up completion of the human genome project because he saw that reading the human genome was less a biology problem than a computer problem. Filippo Brunelleschi is known today as the architect of Florence's magnificent Duomo, but it was his professional experience as a clockmaker that enabled him to create the machinery—the winches, cranes, and hoists—needed to construct the first great building of the Renaissance.[4] Crossover experience, like multiple intelligences, emotions, and imagination, is a resource that finds a natural home in both artistic and economic flows; as notions like crossover and duality suggest, the business world can benefit substantially by enhancing its economic models with artistic elements.

Artistic resources are found in people rather than on balance sheets, and their abundance makes them inimical to strict accounting. Economic resources, which are scarce by definition, are much easier to keep track of. In business, we know which human resources we employ and what we are paying for them. All these people have emotions, experience, imagination, and artistic intelligence. It wouldn't cost us more to tap into these underused resources, but they generally aren't lying out in plain view. We need a framework to account for artistic resources as explicitly as the "dismal science" accounts for economic ones.

Artistic Processes in Business

In between the upstream inputs and the downstream outputs, in between resources and desires lie all the processes that connect them. In business terms, they are familiar to us as R&D, manufacturing, distribution, sales, and marketing, and as corporate overhead functions like finance and human resources. Together, these processes transform resources into products and services. Raw materials get refined, parts get assembled, and products get shipped, either physically or electronically. Collectively, the processes are referred to as a value chain.

You can think of the links in the value chain as coming in various orders. A good rule is to start with the customer, so marketing might be the first step. Alternatively, the flow might begin with research and development. If your business is a restaurant like Chez Panisse that uses only fresh, locally grown produce, you might start with purchasing, since what you sell would depend on what you could find in the market that morning. In any case, the processes in the economic flow are somewhat similar. Each process takes as its inputs the outputs of the preceding process. Each process can be evaluated in terms of its efficiency— the ratio of value created to value consumed.

The artistic flow of business has its own version of the value chain, in which the processes are create ▶ produce ▶ connect.

Create, the first of the three processes, is where the magic happens. Creating begins with a hunch, an idea, an observation. Beethoven always kept a notebook with him and was constantly jotting down musical ideas that he might want to use. Once you've got an interesting hunch, it's time to collect materials to flesh it out and to immerse yourself in them. Car companies with headquarters in Michigan, Japan, and Germany have design labs in Southern California, where new trends appear and early adopters live. If you are trying to stay ahead of other innovators, you need to immerse yourself in the environment where the early adopters live and where trends make their first appearances.

Creating something new requires leaps of imagination. After having a hunch and immersing yourself in source materials, things need time to simmer, connect, and sort themselves out. Then, with a little luck, somewhere along the way a miracle happens, that *Click!* moment when everything falls into place. "Aha! I think I'll paint a woman with no eyebrows and just a hint of a smile!"

But there's more to creating than getting the big idea. The *Click!* sometimes happens before any paint goes on the canvas. More often it happens well after the work has begun. Execution is not the grunt work of the creative process. Execution is where skill and experience come into play. Lots of people have creative ideas; artists have the "chops" to bring them to life.

Produce, getting work in front of audiences, is as important in the artistic flow as getting products to customers is in the economic flow. Both start with the daily work that makes great performances possible. Artists, however, practice every day, keeping in shape, making sure that their technical skills don't get sloppy over time. Business types practice too, but they rarely bring the same day-in-day-out discipline to it.

In a performance all the parts come together, and the piece is ready to be judged by its audience, or the offer by its customers. People are "performing" in the sense that they are delivering the best possible rendering of the work. Jan Carlzon, when he was the CEO of Scandinavian Airlines System almost two decades ago, completely turned around the company's fortunes by focusing on what he called "moments of truth," those 50,000 times a day when a customer interacted directly with someone from the airline. Pilots, flight attendants, baggage handlers, and sales agents came to see that moments in their jobs called for a great performance.

Connect, the third artistic process, involves the audience as much as the artist, the customer as much as the creator and producer. In fact, when art touches audience members, they become artists themselves. The audience's work in creating art goes beyond encountering a piece and responding to it. It also includes sharing that experience with other people. In doing so, the audience is not only marketing the work, it is contributing to its creation.

Encountering art isn't passive. Our response can take the form of laughter, applause, or, at the art museum, respectful murmurs. Applause and other outbursts communicate an audience's appreciation to performers and allow people to express their emotions. At the great Kabuki Theater in Tokyo, the audience has its favorite characters and calls out its advice and emotional reactions to the highly stylized and scripted situations. It's startling to see and hear the normally reserved Japanese spectators shouting out the equivalent of "Kill the bum" in the midst of the action on stage. It shows how engaging the art form is.

Success, so the saying goes, has many fathers, while failure is an orphan. When consumers start telling their friends what they made of a performance, they are really explaining how it touched them, how it became part of their lives. In business, it is said that the customers own a brand, because they decide what it means to them. In art, the audience "owns" the artwork, as long as it was good enough to truly touch them.

Although economic and artistic processes have similarities and overlaps—both take raw materials and then transform and deliver them—the two also differ significantly. Economic processes are large scale and collective; artistic processes are as often as not personal. Economic processes are judged by how efficiently they operate; artistic processes are judged by the quality of the product. Making both business and art work is a matter of creating value, performing effectively, and connecting with the customer. Economic and artistic flows are different ways of fulfilling the audience's desires.

Artistic Outputs in Business

Downstream, at the end of each flow, are the outputs, what business delivers to its customers to fulfill their desires and provide a satisfying customer experience. Customers have economic desires in mind when they evaluate different offers in terms of what is better, faster, cheaper, and safer.

Better is when James Dyson, the British inventor, built a better (i.e., bagless) vacuum cleaner that sucks up half a billion dollars a year in worldwide sales. *Faster* is when

The Elements of Artistic Flow

Moore's Law makes computing and connecting ever faster, creating expectations that every business will work more quickly, too. *Cheaper* is when outsourcing a call center to Bangalore lowers costs. *Safer* is when buyers pay a premium for Ralph Lauren clothing that reduces the chance of product flaw and aesthetic mishap.

While our economic desires emphasize effectiveness and efficiency, our artistic desires emphasize emotional and aesthetic needs. The natural consequence is that different values rise to the fore. Again and again, we run into qualities we look for in art that can also enrich business.

Beauty is generally the first thing people look for in art. It elicits admiration and delight for itself, without any consideration of its usefulness. Imagine how much more wonderful something beautiful is when it also serves its purpose perfectly. Apple's iPod is beautiful to look at, and, even more important, its software and user interface are beautiful to use. The beauty lies in the product itself and in the effect it produces. In its July 26, 2004, cover story, *Newsweek* gushed, "iPod, Therefore iAm." Finding and recognizing beauty is important in all sorts of work. The ballplayer makes a beautiful catch, the mathematician admires a beautiful equation, the retailer pines for a beautiful selling season, and a parent praises a child for a beautiful report card.

Excitement is often the inverse of beauty. A piece of art

can be compelling without being beautiful in a conventional sense. Great tragedies and good horror movies are engrossing because of the physiological sense of relief we get when they're over. The raucous percussion of Stravinsky's *Rite of Spring* touched off a riot at its premiere in 1913, and ninety years later it still stirs up an aesthetic connection with the listener. Excitement is an emotional need and an aesthetic quality. Even a commodity item like salt can have the spice of excitement. In David's kitchen cabinet you'll find several different types of salt: not just Morton's ("When it rains, it pours"), but also Diamond kosher salt and two different sea salts, Maldon flakes from England and Fleur de Mer crystals from Brittany. The gourmet salts sell for ten to twenty times the price of the unexciting commodity.

Enjoyment is a brighter and lighter aesthetic quality. It is more an art form than an economic form. Whenever we take pleasure or satisfaction in an experience or possession, we're expressing an aesthetic value. Watching an old episode of *The Honeymooners* is an aesthetic experience, if only because it's so funny. Enjoying a good meal, a pleasant conversation, a terrific bargain, or a huge advantage can have an aesthetic profile. "Living well is the best revenge" has its own ironic aesthetic. When was the last time you enjoyed a plane ride, a doctor's office visit, or calling the phone company with a service question? Businesses that pay attention to providing enjoyment to their customers add value to their basic offer. It's a shame that so many businesses, and even entire industries, consider enjoyment irrelevant. Imagine the competitive advantage for the one company in each field that gives this even the slightest nod. The pleasant surprise could counteract a multitude of sins.

Meaning is another quality with an aesthetic about it. Meaning comes from the psychological significance attached to something more than from the thing itself. The two strangers had a meaningful encounter, the adversaries had a meaningful negotiation, and the executive had a meaningful job. Dr. Viktor Frankl survived three years in Nazi concentration camps and wrote in *Man's Search for Meaning* how people experienced their imprisonment and torture. Those who managed the best were able to find meaning in even the most horrible circumstances. "The striving to find a meaning in one's life," wrote Frankl, "is the primary motivational force in man."[5] In his business books, like *The Pursuit of WOW!*, Tom Peters has written about how, why, and when work is ennobling and meaningful.[6]

Artistic desires abound, but right now we'll add just one to the list. *Balance* is another aesthetic impulse we look for in what we buy and how we work. Too much of any good thing ruins the aesthetic. Finding the balance in a duality comes not so much from seeking the middle road or splitting the difference as from embracing a duality's contrasts and complementarities. Brooks Brothers' program for mass customization, called "digital tailoring," is an example of pursuing universal satisfaction by personalizing the experience. The clothing is simultaneously made-to-measure and mass produced, balancing customization and cost control.

When customers look for solutions to their needs, they express artistic desires and economic desires. When we see how fundamental and widely held artistic desires are, it becomes clear that they can connect creators and customers in new, richer ways.

The Duality of the Two Flows

To most of us, the economic flow is more familiar than the artistic flow. Yet, emotions and imagination are as real as labor and capital, creating and connecting are as real as manufacture and sales, and beauty and meaning are as real as fast and cheap. So why do we have such difficulty embracing artistic elements and integrating them into a richer, blended flow?

One reason is that economic flow is relatively easy to quantify, while artistic flow is qualitative. Where the former is more objective, the latter is more subjective. Desires in the artistic flow, for instance, describe what we are looking for in our lives as a whole and not just in a piece of art. We don't want our lives to be faster or cheaper, but we do want them to be more meaningful. Marketing and sales people become more effective when they expand their vocabulary and sensibility to speak to artistic elements as well as economic ones.

When people focus too much on quantifiable inputs, outputs, and processes because they are easier to make sense of, they can lose sight of their real goals, such as quality. Seeing only the economic flow, managers think of quality in terms of a low error rate. Total quality management means zero defects. Six sigma, the holy grail of the quality movement, means no more defects than one part per million. The work that W. Edward Deming began in postwar Japan came to its logical conclusion with Ray Kroc at McDonald's: every Big Mac today is just as good as every other Big Mac.

The pursuit of artistic quality is completely different. Accuracy in the arts is a means to an end. Why else do musicians practice their scales, and dancers their steps? But on the other hand, a flawless performance is by no means perfect. Take the first of the Bach Two-Part Inventions, for example. Note after note flows into a stream of sixteenth notes, with a few trills and a couple of longer notes. The more accurately you can play it, the better it is. Right? Wrong.

Act One: See with Both Eyes

For under a hundred dollars, you can get software for your computer that will play the music flawlessly. Each note is just like the others. Each crescendo starts equally soft and grows equally loud. And the results, as the novelist Colette put it, sound like sewing machine music.[7] In other words, mechanical and soulless, perfect but not very good.

Robert Pirsig's classic road novel, *Zen and the Art of Motorcycle Maintenance*, tells the story of a man's search for quality and truth.[8] He sees that truth can be proven logically using a Socratic dialectic. Quality, he comes to understand, can never be proved, only recognized and worked toward. After about three hundred pages, he decides you can't have both truth and quality; they really are a dichotomy. Then he accuses the great Western thinkers of taking the easy way out: they focus on what they can prove, but they are afraid of quality.

Too many people in business are just as afraid of quality. They pursue what's safe and predictable, as in faster, cheaper, and more reliable. Business wants to make the thing right; art wants to make the right thing. That's why business is efficient, and art is effective. But business folk love to say "We've got to be more effective and efficient"— salt and pepper terms that are seldom seen one without the other—providing strong evidence that artistic and economic approaches can and should go together.

The Elements of Artistic Flow

Artistic quality is not so much about predictability as it is about rightness—the chord that haunts, the phrase that thrills, the movement that enchants, and the scene that lingers. Quality is something you work toward, something you dream of when you swing for the fences.

And it doesn't stop there. Working with the artistic flow can improve the economic flow. Using resources in the artistic flow, like artistic intelligence and experience, enables us to use economic resources more effectively. When we see work as creating—not just as doing—we rethink the value chain and our place in it, both personally and in a specific industry. Satisfying customers' artistic desires is the best way to address their long-term needs, going beyond what they're in the market for today.

Although what's natural comes hard, the two flows aren't at odds. The better we get at one, the better we will find we are at the other. In the next six chapters, we'll show you how to make the elements of artistic flow a more important part of your work and business. The point isn't to appreciate artists' work; it's to make *your* work something others will appreciate more.

See Yourself as an Artist

CHAPTER FOUR

Artistic Inputs in Business

Artistic inputs operate very differently from economic ones. Inputs like land, labor, and capital can be applied in variable amounts, trading off an increase of one for a decrease of another. Artistic inputs like imagination and emotion don't work incrementally. They push things forward in leaps and surprises. They don't obey the laws of calculus, which makes them less likely to show up in an economist's model.

Imagination is an artistic resource, and so is emotion. Intelligence, more particularly artistic intelligence, is a critical raw material, and so is experience. Sure, more things go into making art and working artistically, but looking at these four inputs will give you a good picture of what resources you have at hand and how you can start delivering the artistic outputs your customers want.

Act Two: See Yourself as an Artist

Unlike economic inputs, which are objective and easy to measure, artistic inputs are intangible. They are skills that help us see connections. They are ways of thinking that help us organize all the possibilities in front of us. Not quite paradoxes, they are more like dualities, bristling with artistic tension.

Imagination is the ability to see possibilities, to see what's not there yet. Emotion is the gift not just of feeling but of anticipating feelings in others. Intelligence, in the classroom or on the basketball court, is the knack for reading between the lines and recognizing connections. And experience is the skill of accumulating insights from what you've seen and from what other people have done.

Though some of us are obviously more blessed with these qualities than others, we all possess them to a degree. Moreover, these resources exist both within the individual and within groups. John Belushi was funny, but the ensemble that created *Saturday Night Live* was even funnier. And because these artistic inputs are both personal and collective, they can grow over time. Because we can build on what others have done before us, our collective intelligence and our collective imagination can continually expand.

In this chapter, we will look at four artistic inputs and the dualities that give them their spark. We do this not because you have to understand them to create art, although that's not a bad idea. Rather, we look closely at these abilities because mastering them gives you a powerful set of tools for the creative and productive work of business.

Imagination: Seeing
What's Not There Yet

Imagination is the ability to see what doesn't exist. It's what prompted George Bernard Shaw (and, later, Bobby Kennedy) to say, "You see things; and you say 'Why?' But I dream things that never were; and I say 'Why not?'" Children have imagination. Geniuses have it. It might take a little imagination to believe that you can find it in your coworkers, but it's there, too.

Children have a wonderful, unselfconscious artistry. A first-grader we know, for example, was asked to write his version of the tale "And to Think That I Saw It on My Way to School." Here's what Adam Rochelle, age seven, wrote.

On my way to School I saw a jet in the sky. A jet in the sky is not so weerd. So I made up a story. I put 12 raindeer poling the jet. But raindeer pol Santuclos. So I put Santa in the jet. But Santa likes to ride his slaye. So I put Santa's slaye with hem in it on the top of the jet. But the jet needs a name. So I named it X52. But sumbuty needs to drive the jet. So I made a elf drive it. No time to think of more I'm almost at school. Wen I got there my teecher asked did you see any thing today. I said, Just a jet in the sky.

The California-based artist Howard Ikemoto tells an often-repeated story about the creativity of children. "When my daughter was about seven years old, she asked me one day what I did at work. I told her I worked at the college—that my job was to teach people how to draw. She stared back at me, incredulous, and said, 'You mean they forget?'"[1]

There's a reason children are so much better than the rest of us at translating their imagination into creativity. They don't yet have internal filters telling them their work might not be good enough to show other people. They aren't afraid of their own imagination.

When inventors flex their imagination, they often take an existing capability and use it in a new setting. Bose's noise cancellation headphones are that kind of invention. These three-hundred-dollar headphones block out most background noise by adding extra sound to what you hear. You might remember from high-school physics how two patterns of waves can cancel each other out if they are mirror images of each other. The engineers at Bose saw the possibilities for doing just that with sound waves. So when you are in a plane and listening to music, you'll find that the steady, predictable noise of the engines gets cancelled out and the music doesn't.

Imagination is also the ability to see what you would be left with if you could take away some of what is currently in front of you. Michelangelo, perhaps apocryphally, said that the secret of sculpture is to remove all the marble that obscures the figure beneath.

Imagine a business hotel that did away with the dining room and the night clerk at the same time that it offered higher-quality rooms and speedier check-ins and check-outs. That's exactly what the Formule 1 chain of hotels in France did. They jettisoned many of the elements we associate with business hotels while upping the standards for other elements. By subtracting features, they added value.

It takes as much imagination to work with what you've got as it does to start with a clean sheet of paper. It takes imagination, and a little moxie, to make lemonade when you're stuck with a bunch of lemons. The hardest thing about imagination isn't waiting for inspiration to strike. It's allowing yourself to be ready. Children have no problem dreaming up things that never were, and neither should you. Allowing yourself to say "Why not?" is the first step to seeing possibilities for things that aren't there ... yet. "Imagination," as Albert Einstein said, "is more important than knowledge."

Emotion: Anticipating Feelings

Emotions are so basic to humans' makeup that they manifest in the same ways across all cultures. Psychologist Paul Ekman ruffled the feathers of many anthropologists when he wrote that the facial expressions of people feeling fear are the same in all cultures.[2] The same is also true for anger, sadness, enjoyment, and a host of other human emotions whether in a downtown tribe in New York or Stone Age tribe in New Guinea. These emotions, along with love, surprise, disgust, and shame, are so fundamental that they resist our ability to control them.

What we can do with emotions is recognize them. That's what empathy is, the ability to know how another person feels. How many times have you been traveling and had something go wrong? The airline loses your reservation, or your hotel room is next door to the disco and right over the kitchen. Besides resolution and compensation, what you are looking for is understanding. You want the person on the other side of the counter to acknowledge that you are unhappy. Once that's established, it's a lot easier to work out some sort of solution.

The ability to feel empathy is central to what Daniel Goleman called emotional intelligence.[3] The ability to recognize emotions in other people is as important as mathematical aptitude to success in business, maybe more so. CEOs might think of themselves as the corporate equivalent of Superman, but they are almost never the people in a company with the highest IQs. Instead, they are the people with a gift for connecting with other people, understanding them, motivating them, selling to them.

When Robert Kelley and Janet Caplan looked at Bell Labs in the early 1990s, they found that all the scientists who worked there were very smart.[4] Moreover, they found that the star performers were no smarter than the average ones. But the stars were much better at getting answers to the questions and help on their projects when they needed it. The reason they could do this was that they were more likely to have built up social networks and to draw on them long before they needed to use them. They had the ability and the sense to connect with their peers as people first and as resources later.

If empathy is the ability to recognize people's feelings, then the emotional skill that artists have is the ability to anticipate feelings. Artists have a sense of what kinds of reactions their work is likely to create. In business, good marketing is about selling the sizzle more than the steak. Even though the steak has some intrinsically appealing qualities, like flavor and nutritional value, its emotional appeal is even stronger. Both sales and marketing are as concerned with how the customer feels as with what he thinks. When American Express tells you that "membership has its privileges," they're not expecting you to start keeping a list of those benefits. They do expect you to feel special.

Leadership is an emotional art, from the executive floor to the factory floor. The best leaders are emotionally honest, in touch with themselves, and genuine in how they interact with others. A boss who's truly clueless, on the other hand, isn't necessarily stupid. He's more likely just out of touch, tone-deaf to the way other people are reacting to his words and unable to anticipate how they will react.

The first step to anticipating how people will feel is understanding what they are already feeling. Artists, who are used to trafficking in emotional responses, are often better at this than their corporate counterparts. Put artists and their corporate counterparts together, and you can really learn something.

Lucy Kimbell is a London-based artist who originally studied engineering design and now is blurring the line between management consulting and art.[5] Kimbell's work is often site-specific and uses a company's employees as part of the creative process. At the headquarters of Lever Faberge, she and collaborator Lucy Newman created a set of interactive floor mats that let people vote with their feet—literally—about how their day was going. Walking down the corridor, people saw a mat that said "Bureaucracy got in my way today" or one of several other statements. They could either walk over the mat (voting "yes") or walk around it ("no").

As both the Heisenberg Uncertainty Principle and the Hawthorne Effect would predict, the very act of measuring how people felt about their company changed how they actually felt about their company.[6] Kimbell's project created a real-time management information system that was amusing, original, provocative, and memorable. Although it would be nice if every company could have an artist in residence like Lucy Kimbell, it would be even nicer if an artist in residence were within each one of us.

Emotion is part of every person in your company and every customer you sell to. Therefore it needs to be part of every offer you bring to market. Ask yourself which emotions you are trying to communicate. Ask yourself which emotions your customers have that you are able to satisfy. There's more to emotional intelligence than just empathy, or the ability to react to other people's emotions. It's also what lets you anticipate feelings so you can act in an informed way.

Intelligence: Reading Between the Lines

Intelligence is more than just the verbal and mathematical skills measured by IQ tests and SATs. As mentioned in the previous chapter, Howard Gardner established the notion of multiple intelligences in his 1983 book, *Frames of Mind*. Besides verbal and mathematical intelligences, he identified kinesthetic, spatial, musical, interpersonal, and intra-personal intelligences. All of these intelligences are artistic.

Kinesthetic intelligence is the intuitive understanding of one's body and movement. It's what dancers and athletes have. When we talk about Savion Glover's genius for dance or Michael Jordan's genius for basketball, we are acknowledging that they truly are gifted with unique abilities, with special intelligences.

Spatial intelligence is what enables great architects to visualize spaces in three dimensions in their imaginations. Art students are taught to draw a straight wooden chair by focusing on the negative spaces, the geometric areas between the rungs. Musical intelligence is not found only among musicians. It is the ability to recognize melodies and phrases, to hear many sounds at once and pull out the different lines.

Gardner calls two other types of intelligence the *personal intelligences.* Intrapersonal intelligence is the capacity for self-knowledge and self-awareness. And interpersonal intelligence includes abilities like leadership, nurturing relationships, keeping friends, and resolving conflicts. Gifted leaders, like gifted peacemakers, seem to know the right things to say. They know how to work with people, for better or worse. As Gardner notes, "Both Nelson Mandela and Slobodan Milosevic have a lot of interpersonal intelligence—they just use it differently."[7]

Artistic Inputs in Business

What makes these intelligences artistic is their ability to give some people the edge in creating good work more quickly. Mathematical intelligence might give a person the ability to calculate in his head the yields on long-term bonds, but a more artistic intelligence is needed if he wants to build a business around new pricing models.

Verbal intelligence makes for better storytelling—the heart of any ad campaign and any good resume. Spatial intelligence helps you visualize what a product will look like when somebody is using it. The personal intelligences are the biggest difference between CEOs and analysts in the strategic planning department.

These intelligences show up early in life. But real genius, as Oliver Sachs observed, shows up in children in only a few fields, such as math and chess. It shows up in music performance and, when lightning strikes every century or so, in composition. But you don't see child prodigies in literature or politics or painting. Why is that? Because the fields that child prodigies succeed in rely on abstract, symbolic, or mathematical skills. They don't require social skills, or what performance review forms these days call *people skills.*

If you look at the two great child composers, Mozart and Mendelssohn, you see that their successful early pieces were instrumental. They didn't write great vocal music until they were adults. Apparently it takes longer for geniuses and average Joes alike to learn about people.

Act Two: See Yourself as an Artist

In business, when genius appears in the young, it is more often entrepreneurial than managerial. Bill Gates was a good programmer but a remarkable salesman. Richard Branson showed his entrepreneurial stuff when he founded *Student* magazine while he was in school, and he went on to early success as the man who signed the Sex Pistols to Virgin Records while he was still in his twenties.

Intelligence is the ability to see how the pieces fit and to leap to an understanding of the situation before anybody else does, like Wayne Gretzky skating to where the puck is going to be. In Branson's case, it let him see how changes in the music industry in the late 1970s were going to create new opportunities.

Artistic intelligence is the ability to see the connections that make it possible to create something wonderful. It builds upon imagination, the ability to see what could be. In the artistic flow, intelligence is the ability to connect the dots between what you can see and what you can imagine.

If imagination is the skill of seeing possibilities, intelligence is the keen awareness that enables you to manipulate those possibilities in your head. A good bridge player has the ability to see how the cards are going to be played after the first of the thirteen tricks is played. A good business strategist can take her competitors' likely countermoves into account as she makes her plans.

Especially after something has gone wrong, people talk

about the importance of being able to connect the dots. This knack for seeing how disparate pieces of information are part of a larger picture is the gist of intelligence. The word *intelligence*, in fact, comes from the words in Latin for "between" and "reading." Intelligence, in other words, is the ability to read between the lines.

Experience: Moving along an Artistic Curve

In business circles, when you hear people talk about "moving down the experience curve," they are talking about the relationship between cumulative experience and total costs. The more you do something, the less it costs to do it. This effect was first quantified at Wright-Patterson Air Force Base in 1925. Air Force engineers noticed, then documented, that every time cumulative aircraft production had doubled, the labor required to build a plane went down by 10 to 15 percent.[8] Forty years later, the Boston Consulting Group's Bruce Henderson expanded this notion of the "learning curve" into an "experience curve" that tracks total costs and not just labor hours.

A comparable effect is driven by artistic experience, and we call it the *artistic experience curve.* The more experience you can take advantage of, the more creative you can be.

In other words, the more you've seen, the more ideas you have. While costs go down with more economic experience, connections go up when you have greater artistic experience.

In both experience curves, cumulative experience drives the results. Cumulative economic experience includes the experience gains of your suppliers and distributors. Cumulative artistic experience includes the insights of everybody you learn from.

"Good judgment comes from experience," said Will Rogers, "and a lot of that comes from bad judgment."[9] Experience is the knowledge of what worked and what didn't work. For some people, it's limited to their firsthand experience. For others, it includes what they learn from colleagues and read in books. For artists, experience is like a scrapbook that contains all the things they have ever seen. It's a treasure chest they can come back to again and again as they look for inspiration. When Herman Melville went to sea as a young man, he collected experiences that would resurface in *Moby-Dick*.

Experience is an artistic input that artists consciously accumulate. Young painters might go to Rome, aspiring songwriters to New York. Budding chefs want the experience that can be found only in a three-star French kitchen. Writers are admonished to "write what you know," and the enterprising ones, like Melville, set off into the world to acquire more experiences.

Renaissance Italy, which gave us both visual perspective and double-entry accounting, was the high-water mark of cross-disciplinary brilliance and collective experience. Artists, scientists, and businessmen built on innovations and insights in each other's fields.

Giotto introduced perspective, which added depth to flat medieval drawing. Other techniques emerging at the same time, such as foreshortening and use of the vanishing point, moved Western art ever further away from sacred symbolism and toward artistic realism. Double-entry bookkeeping similarly affected the business world of that era. It was imagined by Fibonacci in 1305 and fully developed by Pacioli in 1494. Pacioli, in fact, was a close friend of Leonardo da Vinci, and the two influenced each other on the interrelationships between mathematics and art.

Pacioli commented, "If you say that music satisfies hearing, one of the natural senses ... [perspective] will do so for sight, which is so much more worthy in that it is the first door of the intellect."[10] Da Vinci, at the time, had only an intuitive sense of proportion and geometry, and Pacioli encouraged him to master concepts like multiples and fractions in order to get proportions exact. Early steps in the mathematics of proportions were used both to advance perspective in art and to quantify and control risk in commerce.

The biggest advance in software in the past ten years didn't come from Microsoft, Sun, or IBM. It came from forty thousand individuals working together to develop the operating system known as Linux. Because nobody owned the intellectual property in the code, everybody was more inclined to contribute to its development. With the mantra "Many eyes reduce complexity," people on opposite sides of the world improved and extended each other's work. In a matter of a few years, this unpaid juggernaut created a powerful, stable operating system that was the first viable threat to Microsoft Windows.

Both Linux and Leonardo drew on the experience of gifted contributors. They were able to move up the artistic experience curve because the collective experience they could draw from made it easier to make creative connections. The curve works because the more you've seen, the more you can imagine.

Most generals (and many spouses) find themselves fighting the last war, unable to see that circumstances may have changed. But if you have the ability to learn from your experiences—and, better still, from others'—you will find that you have more raw materials to work with. Experiences aren't so much mental postcards as they are collected insights waiting to be put together and set to work. Experience links wisdom garnered from the past into a duality with creativity that sees the future.

We should also add that while we speak of experience as an input people use in their work and business, experience is also an outcome. In *The Experience Economy*, Joe Pine and Jim Gilmore say that "you are what you charge for," and that work is theater and every business is a stage.[11] In their memorable example, coffee costs a few pennies a cup when it's bought and sold on the commodities exchange; it's anywhere from five to twenty-five cents a cup when you buy a can of coffee; the price goes up to fifty cents or a dollar when you buy it in a cup; and when you buy coffee in a café or restaurant, you pay between two and three dollars a cup. The experience and the pricing are different at each point in this economic flow; and the outcome, the experience, can cost a hundred times more than the coffee.

Finding Artistic Resources at Work

For an employer, finding a person with the right set of abilities and experiences is harder than scanning a few hundred resumes. The way that the arts world searches for and selects talent is different from that of the business world, and, in some ways, it is probably better.

Artists understand that some people have got it, and others don't, where the *it* in question is talent—one part gift and two parts grit. Depending on the art form, an artist's performing years are numbered, so directors are always looking for fresh talent. Unlike their counterparts in the business world, directors are constantly on the prowl, looking for the next big talent that's going to come along. The same way that Silicon Valley is good at R&D, the arts world is good at scouting talent.

When the New York Philharmonic is filling a vacant chair, it invites a number of superb players to audition on stage. They play their audition pieces seated behind a curtain, so the judges can't see them play. Their music, not their resumes or pretty faces, must speak for them. When orchestras look for new directors, the auditions take the form of guest conductor appearances. Before the new conductor is hired, everybody has heard how well he works with the orchestra.

Contrast this with the way large corporations look for new CEOs. As Rakesh Khurana described in his book *Searching for a Corporate Savior*, firms typically hire an executive search company like Russell Reynolds or Spencer Stuart to find the two or three best candidates from outside the firm.[12] They look for people with experience running a company at least as large and preferably more prestigious—but not people with experience working in the firm itself. The unfortunate result is that CEOs are hired for their "charisma" and their reputation with Wall Street, for the appearance of talent instead of for the real thing. The *Fortune* 500 could learn a thing or two from the arts groups they underwrite.

Finding people who bring the right mix of artistic inputs—imagination, emotion, intelligence, and experience—is more important than finding people with the right resumes. These skills balance what's real with what could be real. The ability to see possibilities, anticipate feelings, recognize connections, and accumulate insights distinguishes an artist from a hack. And these inputs are found not just in individuals but in groups. So creating an environment where artistic inputs can develop is as important as finding the people who already have them.

In the artistic flow of business, these four capabilities are the fuel for the processes that ultimately satisfy customers' needs for beauty, excitement, enjoyment, and meaning. Artistic inputs like these make possible the artistic complement to economic work.

CHAPTER FIVE

Tell Your Story, Write Your Poem, Sing Your Song

In the last chapter we focused on artistic resources or inputs that complement economic ones and enrich the standard elements of running a business. Emotion, imagination, artistic intelligence, and experience contribute significantly to carrying out regular business tasks. In this chapter we're going to look at some specific ways to put these qualities into action. Our purpose is to be suggestive rather than complete, to show how real artistic acts can be

applied to real business problems. We've chosen three artistic acts—storytelling, poetry, and song—that can be creatively applied in business settings.

Tell Your Story

When Louis Gerstner took over as CEO at IBM in the early 1990s, the company was sinking like a stone. One of the first decisions he made was to continue offering System/390, the company's mainframe servers, which, together with software that ran on them, represented over 90 percent of IBM's profits. In his autobiography, *Who Says Elephants Can't Dance?*,[1] Gerstner describes one of his first meetings:

> At that time, the standard format of any important IBM meeting was a presentation using overhead projectors and graphics on transparencies that IBMers called—and no one remembers why—"foils." Nick [Donofrio, who was then running the System/390 business] was on his second foil when I stepped to the table and, as politely as I could in front of his team, switched off the projector. After a long moment of awkward silence, I simply said, "Let's just talk about your business."
>
> I mention this episode because it had an unintended, but

terribly powerful, ripple effect. By that afternoon an e-mail about my hitting the Off button on the overhead projector was crisscrossing the world. Talk about consternation! It was as if the President of the United States had banned the use of English at White House meetings.

Gerstner didn't want his lieutenant to show him a presentation. He wanted to know what the unvarnished truth was. What he didn't expect was that switching off the projector would become a story in its own right.

Events that become "stories" take on a life of their own. Their popularity is a truer barometric reading of what people think and feel than any formal statement. They make the subtext tangible and memorable. In the case above, for example, IBM's economic decision involved drastically lowering prices to compete effectively; the switch turn-off story artfully got at the truth that things were going to change dramatically. The story had a far greater effect than did any management edict.

Stories in business and work are part of the artistic flow that adds nuance and life to the dry daily chatter of the rational economic stream. They don't have to be made up. They just happen, and the first skill is to recognize a good story. Good stories tell a simple, recognizable truth and have an underlying moral that goes well beyond the narrative. They capture precisely those qualities that formal presentation and decision-making leave out.

Great leaders often make the best storytellers, whether in business, politics, religion, or entertainment. In every realm, storytellers blend the personal and the universal. In business, they combine the ideas that capture people's minds with the personal force that captures people's hearts. Whatever your point, it's always most convincing when you marry reason and emotion, economic and artistic flow.

Great storytellers, like Will Rogers, Bill Cosby, and Garrison Keillor, mastered the craft of storytelling and the skills of pacing, character development, and punch lines. Further down the food chain, corporate storytellers add color to conferences and off-sites with their arsenals of leadership sagas and innovation anecdotes. As talented and on the mark as the latter left-brained troubadours may be, however, they are generally little more than garnish, the sprinkled dash of chopped parsley that enlivens a dull plate. The storytellers that really matter are the ones in the offices and cubicles and on the factory floors. They have information they need to communicate, and they can do it more effectively when they use stories instead of turgid Power-Point and cryptic e-mails.

Of all business activities, advertising is the most deeply versed in storytelling. It wouldn't be an exaggeration to say that every good ad tells a story, and that the really terrific ones are little gems, cameo works of art. Take the Master-Card commercials, like the one that ran during the 2004 Super Bowl. "Diapers, milk, and laundry detergent: $25. Routine oil change: $20. Haircut: $75. Getting your errands done quicker to spend more time with your family: priceless." Over the space of thirty seconds, the commercial takes you through the arc of a busy Saturday morning. And this particular commercial used animation and humor to tell its story, showing how even Homer Simpson needs a credit card.

Advertising is a heightened form of communication. It accomplishes what we all would like to accomplish, if we only had the time, the talent, and the budget. Look beyond what the advertisers do to see how they do it. Their tools are basically artistic, emphasizing sound and images much more than numbers and text; they work with emotions more than reason, and they use stories to make their point.

Stories are too valuable, however, to be left only to advertisers. Imagine managers in production, finance, and every other function in your company being as good at storytelling (true stories, not tall tales) as your company's ad agency is. Your company would be awash in artistic flow. And even if it's not a flood at first, it would create a stronger aesthetic trickle in the great economic wash.

Everybody is more effective when they make their

points by telling a story. We're all used to giving examples to support our points. Well, give an example and you're halfway to a story. Add a character, an event, a narrative thread, a punch line, a recognizable truth, an identifiable moment, and you've got a story.

We have a friend, a successful businesswoman, who started working on her communication skills after a lover had let her down. "Between marriages I had this wild, torrid love affair with one of the most fascinating men I've ever met in my life. He knew more people than God. One of the reasons I was so attracted to him is that I basically think of myself as a boring person, a little too earnest. We were in bed on a Saturday morning, about six weeks into this relationship, and he told me a story. I thought, 'Wait a minute, I've heard this story before.' I realized that the most fascinating person I'd ever spent time with had only six weeks' worth of stories, and then he started to repeat them. The reason I thought I was boring was that I'd heard all my own stories. And it wasn't about the content, it was about how I told the stories. So I have spent a lot of time trying to make my storytelling richer."

Many companies have founding myths, stories about how they got their start. Hewlett-Packard was founded in Bill Hewlett's garage in Palo Alto, California, in 1939. The company was named Hewlett-Packard instead of Packard-Hewlett because Dave Packard lost a coin toss. The company's first product success was with a new type of oscilla-tor that Walt Disney bought when he was making *Fanta-sia*. HP's founding myths are known today by virtually everybody at the company because they communicate the firm's basic values. The garage represents entrepreneurial optimism, the coin toss an attitude of fairness to all em-ployees, and the oscillator the importance of innovation. Although it's theoretically possible to get all those ideas into a mission statement that fits neatly onto one Power-Point slide, why bother, when storytelling does a better job keeping the message alive.

Stories like HP's package people's experience to make an emotional connection. You draw on the artistic re-sources around you and weave facts together in a way that makes them art. It's an effective way of transforming re-sources into results.

Write Your Poem

Poetry and business, in most people's eyes, are two com-pletely different worlds. According to the stereotypes, po-ets dress badly and drink espresso, while businessmen dress well and drink double decaf lattes. But some poets work both sides of the street. John Barr, former investment banker and now president of the wealthy Poetry Founda-tion (recipient of a $100 million endowment gift in 2002), is one of them. "In both of these fields," he said, "you use creativity to find order in a chaotic experience. Business does that in the external world. Poetry does it internally by way of articulation."[2]

Dana Gioia, currently the chairman of the National Endowment for the Arts, is a Stanford MBA who spent fifteen years working in the corporate world. In 1991, when he was a Vice President of Marketing at General Foods, he published his second book of poetry, *The Gods of Winter.*[3] Here's one of the poems in it that we particularly like:

M O N E Y

Money, the long green,
cash, stash, rhino, jack
or just plain dough.

Chock it up, fork it over,
shell it out. Watch it
burn holes through pockets.

To be made of it! To have it
to burn! Greenbacks, double eagles,
megabucks and Ginnie Maes.

It greases the palm, feathers a nest,
holds heads above water,
makes both ends meet.

Act Two: See Yourself as an Artist

Money breeds money.
Gathering interest, compounding daily.
Always in circulation.

Money. You don't know where it's been,
but you put it where your mouth is.
And it talks.

That same year, Gioia wrote an essay in *The Atlantic Monthly* that made him famous. In "Can Poetry Matter?" he argued that poetry used to be read and written regularly by educated people in our country, but all that stopped when poets started writing only for other poets.[4] We agree. Poetry is too important to be left to poets. It would be much better if it belonged to everyone, producers and consumers alike. In work and business, poetry could be a powerful tool for deepening reason and logic through the use of emotion and imagination.

Marrying poetry to business may not seem like a logical or simple task, but the stretch is worth the effort. That's what a great advertising jingle does: "You'll wonder where the yellow went, when you brush your teeth with . . ." Get businesspeople to put their thoughts into a poem, and they're likely to express what they really think more truthfully, clearly, compellingly, and succinctly than they might if they wrote about the same topic in more traditional business-ese. Just getting them to do it, of course, stretches the imagination.

Babson College, in Wellesley, Massachusetts, is doing exactly that. Ten years ago this business school for entrepreneurs got feedback from corporations looking to hire its graduates that the students weren't comfortable with uncertainties and ambiguities, that they weren't willing to take risks. The faculty believed creativity was lacking in the school's programs and graduates, so they launched a "Creativity Stream" at the beginning of their MBA program, later extending it into an executive distance-learning program, which they run for Intel Corporation.

Over time they discovered what works best—a mix that now includes poetry, fiction writing, puppetry, improvisation, movement, and music. A dance professor teaches people to move rhythmically rather than dance, and the music instructor has people build their own instruments from junkyard materials.

All hundred and fifty or so entering students have to take the program. They are randomly assigned, so they can't just work on an art form with which they're familiar. In the spirit of the exercise, they're asked to switch groups if this happens. At the end of the module, each ten-person team decides on its own venue and presents its work during a two-day event to which the entire community is invited.

Act Two: See Yourself as an Artist

The program is directed by an engaging poet, Mary Pinard. "We're not making musicians," she says, "but rather helping them to understand the creative process, risk taking, ambiguity, trust, and community building in a way that they can't obstruct. They have to move through it so they can do a presentation."[5]

They used to give scores and prizes at Babson but learned almost immediately that this MBA-like way of doing things was wrong for understanding how creativity works. Now, they're very clear that the evaluation criteria involve things like emotional, physical, intellectual, and psychological presence, responsibility to the group, and success at community building.

The faculty works with "students that don't yet have aesthetics or creativity on their radar screens," Pinard says, "and they're certainly not expecting to encounter these in an MBA program. So I can shock them on a very basic level and force them to experience it. They wouldn't do it without the structure, the requirement, and the permission. We're planting an impulse."

Babson's program isn't about "thinking outside of the box." Pinard has a clearer, more original view. "What our creativity module has to offer businesspeople is a passion for realizing a vision, a personal urgency to express something."

After the first module, the class is much tighter and more

willing to take risks with one another. "The creative work ends up revealing something about who you are, how you grasp principles," says one student. Ultimately, that translates into better projects and a deeper sense of purpose, into getting in touch with a part of yourself that you thought was dead.

Poetry can also help you get in better touch with the people around you. A simple game that Stan and his family play lets them express themselves by writing poems together. They take turns writing the lines and then, when the poem is finished, naming it together. We say *game* because it's done as fun, as evening entertainment, or to dissipate the boredom of a long car drive. It can be done orally or on paper. No one has to feel they're "a poet." Here is a short example:

SKIPPING

I can skip to the corner.
I can skip to the moon.
I can skip stones and rainbows.
I can skip school and family feuds.
But if I skip lines and stitches,
My poem will unravel.

No maximum or minimum word or line limits exist, and you can make up your own rules and variations as you go, such as changing poets mid-line or writing a few lines before stopping if it feels right. This is best played by two people at a time, to begin with, but you can add more contributors once you have gone a few rounds in duos. Two can often be more playful or intimate and may involve a conversation, as in this poem:

FANCY FOOTWORK

"I want to put my foot here," *he said.*
   "Where?" *she asked.*
"Here," *he said, suggesting his toe to her* mouth.
   "Why?" *she asked.*
"So you won't be too noisy when
I put my other foot there," he said.

We include these two playful, nonbusiness poems to say that everybody can write poems. Paradoxically, most of us think both that business is too serious to fool around with poetry, and that poetry is too serious to enter into our daily life. We're talking not about the Nobel Prize for Literature but about how to enhance business perspectives by introducing artistic elements.

In a work setting, shared poem writing serves equally well as a way for new project members to get to know each other, to begin the task by having fun, and to express emotions that might otherwise stay unconscious. Brainstorming, conflict resolution, feedback sessions, job searches, office relations, focus groups, new product development, best practices benchmarking, and corporate branding all lend themselves to poetic form.

Applying resources that too often go unused, in this case artistic intelligence and imagination, makes it possible to get more accomplished than if you draw only on the economic resources at hand. Taking what needs to be said and distilling it into the most evocative form is the difference between the mundane and the musical.

Sing Your Song

Walt Whitman saw the poetry and music that exist in the workaday world. One of his poems in *Leaves of Grass* captures the sense of dignity, beauty, and meaning that all sorts of people find in their work.

I HEAR AMERICA SINGING

I hear America singing, the varied carols I hear,
Those of mechanics, each one singing his as it should be
blithe and strong,
The carpenter singing his as he measures his plank or beam,

The mason singing his as he makes ready for work, or leaves
off work,

The boatman singing what belongs to him in his boat, the
deckhand singing on the steamboat deck,

The shoemaker singing as he sits on his bench, the hatter
singing as he stands,

The wood-cutter's song, the ploughboy's on his way in the
morning, or at noon intermission or at sundown,

The delicious singing of the mother, or of the young wife at
work, or of the girl sewing or washing,

Each singing what belongs to him or her and to none else,

The day what belongs to the day—at night the party of
young fellows, robust, friendly,

Singing with open mouths their strong melodious songs.

It's possible to imagine the laborers and artisans of a hundred years ago singing while they worked. The shoemaker could sing at his bench, and nobody would hear the wood-cutter in the forest. But what about white-collar workers in today's workforce? It's not often that we hear corporate America singing these days. But a few voices are out there.

We first got an inkling of different ways to use music and song as a business resource some years ago, when a senior executive brought us a tape recording he wanted us to hear. On it was some reasonably pleasant jazz, a piano player with guitar and woodwind accompaniment. "That's really nice.

Who is it?" we asked, naturally. "That's me on piano," the executive said with a pleased smile. "But you don't play the piano!" "That's what's so amazing," he replied, and he went on to tell us about a two-day music seminar he attended.

It sounded so good, we took it the next time it was offered. Ronald Heifetz, a professor at Harvard's Kennedy School of Government, ran the seminar and played cello. The seminar included two other musicians and a technician who recorded everything. At the end, participants received a tape of their individual contributions. Through the years, Heifetz integrated his musical material into his courses on leadership.

The seminar's premise was that music is a means of communication that resides in everyone. Some of us are trained in its techniques while others are not, but it's there nevertheless. Melody and rhythm are universals, possibly even in our genes. The goal of the seminar was to bring out the musicality that is within and to connect with others through the music.

The only prep work was to bring a poem or short piece of writing that we would read aloud. Heifetz said we should each read the piece that we brought, then "sing your song." He didn't explain what that meant, only that it was to come from within and follow naturally from the reading.

Stan read the poem "Reflections on a Gift of Water-melon Pickle . . ." by John Tobias. The poem began, "During that summer / When unicorns were still possible." It evoked a time that may never have happened but which, through the poem, became more real than the one that is: a time when watermelons ruled. The musicians picked up the cadence in the poem, and Stan's song skipped childlike down that summer morning.

A fortyish woman read Robert Frost's "The Road Not Taken" and then gathered her composure to sing her song. We all waited expectantly. You could see she was going deeply into herself, struggling to begin.

What came out of her was otherworldly and profoundly disturbing and off-putting. It was an agonizing wail, a primal screamsong. Without realizing it, she was singing her deepest emotions for us, sharing a premature intimacy that might have been reserved for only her therapist and husband. After the first few bars, the musicians softly began to accompany her. What started as an embarrassment that was too personal to hear became something shared and universal.

After two days of such musical exercises, we ended the seminar with each of us picking a few notes at the piano, getting the musical backup and beat, finding a groove, and knowing, yes, yes, music is in all of us and is a wonderful way to communicate.

Tell Your Story, Write Your Poem, Sing Your Song

We went back to thank our friend who had introduced us to the seminar, and he said, "I know. It's just amazing. After I took the seminar, I had to make a sales call to the president of a firm. I didn't know him, and he was very intimidating. I didn't know how to begin, so I just said, 'Why don't we sing a song together, first.' Well, he was taken aback but then got into it, and by the end of the song we were friends before I even started trying to sell to him." That's a true story.

We thought this story was one of a kind, fun but weird and not something others would do, but we were wrong. An entrepreneur, financier, and longtime patron of the arts, for example, told us, "My interest in the arts has always taken me into metaphors or songs. In a business context, I'll often say to people, 'We've seen this before, we can write a song about that.' Then I'll sing a few bars of 'We've been in this place before.' I literally do that, I do it often, and I have people do it back to me. It brings people to another place and connects us at a different, deeper level."

Ruminating further, he continued, "It deepens the emotional meaning of our relationship, expands our bandwidth. It often moves the conversation, causing the person to speak more meaningfully. Part of what I'm doing is saying 'I can understand that.' It's such a universal experience that we write songs about such things. My experience in the arts has given me a much broader range of metaphors."

Act Two: See Yourself as an Artist

As our entrepreneur friend knows, drawing on artistic intelligence can work in business; it's fun and it's more effective. When we make the jump from speech to song, we tap into the intuition that makes connections faster than our logical minds do, and we can exploit the imagination that sees how things could someday be. Using our artistic resources helps us get done what needs to be done and helps us to leave our mark when we have gone.

Warren Senders begins his classes at the New England Conservatory of Music by asking his students, "What happened to you musically this week?" When we were there, a young woman said she volunteers regularly at a nursing home. That week she had encountered a very upset elderly woman who had soiled herself and couldn't get the staff to change her because they were too busy. The girl held her hand and quietly began to sing "Amazing Grace." Soon, the woman joined in and within a few minutes had forgotten how upset she was, by which time the attendant arrived to help. A young man in Senders's class said that he was on a bus holding his percussion instruments and noticed a little child staring at them. He showed the child some of the noises they made, and he had the child make them. Shortly other passengers chimed in, tapping and clapping. When the child got up to leave with his mother, he asked, "Can I take music lessons?"

Tell Your Story, Write Your Poem, Sing Your Song

There's a Zimbabwean expression, "If you can talk, you can sing; if you can walk, you can dance." Try it in your work, your business, your relations, and your life.

What You Can Do

Sing your song, indeed. Write your poem, and use it for the lyrics. Whatever you do, tell your story. You'll feel better for it, and so will the people you work with. You'll discover that your artistry will bring more meaning, beauty, enjoyment, and excitement to your work and your workplace.

In the previous chapter we focused on how to recognize artistic inputs and give legitimacy and importance to things like emotions, imagination, artistic intelligence, and aesthetic experiences in a business context. In this chapter we focused on ways to put those resources to work. Getting yourself started is often difficult, so we offer you these suggestions:

▶ Whatever your job, take a customer's experience with your company's product or service and then find the story in it.
▶ Tell the story several times, each time asking yourself how you can tell it better without changing its truthful-

ness. Tell your coworkers and your boss, your friends and your family. Keep telling the story until you've got it nailed and people light up upon hearing it.

▶ As Harvard Business School professor Ben Shapiro once said, if you want to know a process, "staple yourself to an order."[6] This is a marvelous device for telling a story —"You'll never guess where I was sent next!"—or writing a poem. Make each stanza another step in the process, and be sure you end by expressing what you learned. We will cover process in detail in the next chapter.

▶ Take a problem you're working on as part of your job and express it artistically in several different ways: as a story, as a poem, as a song, as a drawing, as a dance. Do this for yourself, not necessarily to show to others, and don't labor long on any one of these attempts. It doesn't matter how inept you are; you're immersing yourself in the problem from a supplementary perspective that's different from the usual rational economic analysis.

▶ Take a reasonably important memo or e-mail you've written and sing it before you send it. Sure, you'll probably want to do it in a room where no one will hear you, and that's fine. What kind of song does it sound like— ballad, oratorio, swing, rap, Gregorian chant, or pep rally cheer? Notice the parts you like and don't like, where you're putting in feeling, emphasis, volume, passion, tempo, mood. The reason for doing this is to get a bead on the nonrational, noncognitive, unconscious reactions the readers-recipients are likely to have. Are they the reactions you want?

▶ If you and another person at work are a little stiff or wary of each other, you aren't connecting, ask this person to indulge you for a few minutes with an experiment. Say that you've got this song in your head, and you'd like some help completing it. You can say you know it sounds goofy or bizarre, but you find it helps you bust through a problem when you put it in song. Be light about it. The song matters not at all; pulling off the experience and connecting on a more meaningful wavelength is what you're after.

If you like any of these ideas and still feel awkward about actually doing them, do them first in the shower . . . over and over . . . until you're ready to try them with others.

See Your Work
as a Work
of Art

CHAPTER SIX

Artistic Processes in Business

Between inputs and outputs are the processes that get us from one end of the flow to the other. The economic processes are R&D, manufacturing, distribution, and marketing. The artistic processes create something, produce and present it, and then connect with the audience: "create ▶ produce ▶ connect." Our purpose in this chapter is to comment on artistic elements in each process and show how they can enrich these business basics.

The creative process, in art and in business, is where the breakthroughs happen, but they don't happen by magic. As choreographer Twyla Tharp describes in *The Creative Habit*, there is a discipline to creativity.[1] A series of activities almost always happen in order. Creativity isn't so much a flash of genius as it is the duality of *managed inspiration*.

Producing a work, getting it ready for its audience, is a matter of practice and rehearsal. It requires both preparing the piece and preparing the performer. Some people's presence makes their sales pitches sing and their presentations compel. This type of genius doesn't just happen; it's the result of hard work and careful preparation. Producing electrifying work is a matter of *practiced presence*.

The final step in the artistic process is not when the artists present their work to their audiences. Instead, it's when the energy from the creator is matched by the energy from the consumer, when they listen to each other, play off each other. Connecting, the final process, is an *energy exchange*.

All three processes in the artistic flow hold dualities that give them their resonance: managed inspiration, practiced presence, and energy exchange. These three, taken together, represent not an alternative way to do the work of business so much as an alternative way to see what really matters in the work that you are doing. The work of transforming inputs to outputs becomes easier, more interesting, and more effective when it draws on both the artistic and the economic processes.

Managed Inspiration:

CREATE ▸ Produce ▸ Connect

Creativity is the ability to use your imagination to develop new and original ideas or things. You might think the entire creative process is mystical and unmanageable, but, ironically, that is not the case. In fact, the creative act goes through a set of predictable phases or steps whose treatment is akin to the economic flow—that is, it's rational and predictable. Oddly enough, most of the phases are manageable in the same way that production and consumption processes are, and get this—artists seem to know this better than managers do.

In *Drawing on the Artist Within*, Betty Edwards discusses the work of Hermann Helmholtz, Henri Poincaré, and Jacob Getzels, identifying successive stages in the creative process.[2] What follows is our own take on the stages of creativity.

The creative process begins with an initial hunch, followed by immersion in the idea or thing, a simmering as it comes to life, an inspirational moment when everything clicks, and then the exposition or execution of it all. Only the brief *Click!* moment remains elusive and mysterious to us. The finer the lens we put on the creative process, the more we understand that all but that singular flash are as manageable as are production and consumption.

Act Three: See Your Work as a Work of Art

Ironically, the arts reaffirm Edison's maxim that "genius is 1 percent inspiration and 99 percent perspiration." Most of what passes for creativity is pretty standard sweat and effort. We spend way too much time, print, and energy focused on the one-in-a-million creative geniuses and on the even rarer one-in-a-billion moments a creative genius has. Since our focus here is not on art for art's sake but on what it can teach us about business, we'll leave the blinding moment to the painter, singer, and dancer and concentrate instead on what gets them there.

We know three things about creativity in artists. First, the overwhelming majority of people—and not just creative artists—are capable of doing almost all the phases of creative work if they're willing to put in the time and effort. Even if the brief inspirational flash can't be managed as an economic process, all the other work can. Second, going through the routine actions in the creative process is the surest route to realizing the elusive *Eureka!* moment. Start by following hunches, then immerse yourself in ideas and consciously let them simmer. After an epiphany, systematically check things out; trust but verify. Third, paying attention to the phases in the artistic flow makes it more likely that the one step that is truly artistic—the *Click!*—really will happen.

This process of managed inspiration can make anybody more creative and any firm more productive. Let's take a closer look at the phases that you will need to manage.

Artistic Processes in Business

Hunch. Scientific breakthroughs often occur when there's an exception to a rule. Scientists and stock-market mavens both call these anomalies. In other fields they're called insights. Most people simply call them hunches. We all have intuitive feelings about things. It may be the glimmer of something that catches your mind's eye. It may be noticing the unexpected, redefining the context, the exception proving the rule.

On a trip to Europe, Howard Schultz noticed the abundance of cafés. Unlike their counterparts in the United States, they served a range of drinks that extended beyond regular and decaf. They gave people a comfortable place to sit for as long as they wanted. And they had plenty of customers who were happy to pay a little extra for the experience. Schultz came back home to Seattle and built his hunch into Starbucks.

Stan remembers a professor showing the class a table with numbers but no labels to explain the rows and columns; then he would ask the students how many cases or stories they could create to fit the data. Conversely he would show the class labels and ask how many tests they could develop to best produce the resulting numbers. His point was not about the specifics but about whether people could learn to generate hunches.

Immerse. "You have to take in all the initial materials," says Mikko Nissinen, Artistic Director of the Boston Ballet, "before you start sorting them out and eliminating anything. You want to open yourself up and take as much in as you can without analyzing it."[3]

Creative artists go through life with their sketchpad open. Gershwin was able to take the noise and bustle of Paris, human and automotive, and rework it in his "American in Paris"; Béla Bartók did the same with Hungarian folk songs. A fertile mind, awash in possibilities, has the luxury of eliminating all the ideas that aren't going to work.

Whether you are an artist or a businessperson, preparing for a piece requires you to take on a studentlike role, learning what is on your palette, what materials you have to work with, and what effects you can put together. For an aspiring composer it means learning the voices and the shortcomings of all the instruments. For an ambitious manager it means understanding your firm's core competencies. Rotating through the major business functions might take a while longer than just rising vertically, but it's more likely to create a better manager. In family-owned firms, Junior often starts his career in the shipping department before moving on to sales, production, and finance. The best way to learn about something is to learn how to do it yourself.

Simmer. After you've immersed yourself and before you have a breakthrough is that period when you sift, stir, rearrange, and wonder why it's taking so long to get it right.

Artistic Processes in Business

Whether you're rewriting a sentence five times, reworking the numbers ten times, mixing the colors over and over, hesitating to make a decision, reviewing the alternatives yet again, or calling still another meeting to discuss action plans, you often feel like you're procrastinating. More often than not, this is a necessary phase in the creative process. Wine ages, sauces reduce, concrete cures, and wood used for furniture seasons. Artists fiddle, techies tinker, lawyers vet, and managers evaluate trade-offs. Every field does it, and each has its own word for it. This is how chance favors the prepared mind.

Business operations and software both need a little time to get it right. Everyone knows that you should never buy version 1.0 software unless you like being on the bleeding edge. Software evolves, and it needs time for simmering and debugging. When retailers open their first store in a new country, they usually don't expect it to make money right away. More often, their primary motivation is to climb a learning curve so they can learn about a market and get better over time.

Businesses love Gantt charts that lay out the length of time each phase in a process should take. Imagine one that said, "Days 4–6: simmer." Like a chef with a hunch about a dish he wants to create after considering all possible ingredients for a recipe, there comes the time to choose and simmer, mixing and testing the balance of contributions.

Act Three: See Your Work as a Work of Art

If you get it right, you have that moment when you taste the dish and . . .

Click! This is the most talked about and least understood phase in the creative flow. In mental terms, it's the most artistic and least economic part of the process. It's also the shortest in duration.

Ever since Archimedes shouted "Eureka!" from his bathtub, everyone recognizes the *Aha!* moment, the quick and illuminating creative flash. Epiphanies happen when you're deeply immersed and simmering in the middle of your work. Sometimes they are anticipated, but more often than not they sneak in when least expected. As John Lennon said, life is what happens when you're making other plans.

You can't really plan for an epiphany; what you can do is recognize one when you have it. Some epiphanies are realizations, like what St. Paul experienced on the road to Damascus. Others are realizations of what could be, like Jackson Pollock's life-changing moment when he first recognized the energy and beauty of his paint dribbled on canvas.

The nationwide limo service Boston Coach got started because Ned Johnson, then CEO of Fidelity Investments, noticed that a lot of cars were being used to drive his managers around. Why not make a business out of it? Fidelity knew how to use information technology to leverage its capital more effectively than the competitors could, and it was already generating enough demand to get the business launched.

The most frequent kind of epiphany is the retrospective epiphany. It's the recognition of what you just did, the enjoyable and embarrassing realization that you didn't know you were having an epiphany, when you really were. By the time you notice it, it's already happened.

Verify. Great! So you've had an epiphany. Too bad that's not enough. Just having a great idea doesn't qualify as creativity. Now you've got to vet your big idea. The mathematician Poincaré, no stranger to big ideas, emphasized the importance of checking ideas for usefulness and mistakes by fleshing them out into concrete form.

Creativity does not mean a straight line from idea to completion. Unless you're a Franz Schubert who never rewrites a note, creativity occurs through trial and error. Thomas Edison was familiar with both trial and error, with both idea and execution. Once, asked to explain an experiment that had flopped, he said that he had not failed at all —he had simply learned one more way that things didn't work. Ironic, isn't it, that *execution* has two meanings, to do and to kill?

Creativity doesn't begin and end with the *Aha!* It starts with a hunch, develops through exploration and simmering, crystallizes in an insight, and is turned into something real through patient, steady effort. The creative process has a flow, and you have no reason to pin your hopes on accidental inspiration when you can find creativity in managed innovation.

Practiced Presence:

Create ▸ **P R O D U C E** ▸ Connect

Steve Jobs, one of the great creative CEOs, likes to point out that "great artists ship." They get the work done, out the door, in front of an audience, and into consumers' hands.

More formally, production encompasses things like procurement, manufacturing, and logistics; further downstream the consumption process includes functions like marketing, distribution, delivery, and customer relations. The process is about making an idea real and getting it to the people who can use it. In the economic flow, production is part of the value chain. In the artistic flow, the same is true but with more emphasis on the presentation.

Great leaders, like great dancers, bring electricity to their performances. They can simply walk into a room, and all the attention shifts to them. They exude a commanding presence. Their aura speaks for them and makes whatever they say or do important to hear. Their performance, their interaction with the others in the room, begins before they even say anything.

It would be misleading to call this ability a gift. It comes from years of practice that prepares them for moments of peak performance. Producing great performances takes practiced presence.

An old joke begins with a passenger asking the cab driver, "Hey, buddy, do you know how to get to Carnegie Hall?" and the cabbie replies, "Yeah, practice." In business, you don't see many people practicing. Yes, we get training, like college or business school or those training workshops we all are sent to once in a while. But how often do you see people working on their basic skills, like speaking, writing, negotiating, selling, or mentoring? Not very often at all. In a world of just-in-time and learning-by-doing, it takes a pretty rare person to carve out the time to work regularly on basic skills.

You'll sometimes see people preparing, but that's not the same thing as practicing. Before a big sales call, they plan out their offer and how they will counter the likely objections. Before a big presentation, managers get all their PowerPoint slides in order and check all the figures. Then they run through their speech in a perfunctory monotone, focusing more on microphone levels and catching mistakes than on tone, impact, phrasing, or delivery quality. What's going on is more planning than practicing, more economic than artistic.

The difference between successful artists and unsuccessful artists isn't just talent. It's also how much time they spend practicing, both in their youth and as adults. Young ballerinas spend three or four hours a day in class, stretching, doing work on the barre, repeating basic steps again and again. That way, when they perform they'll be able to do things well, do things the right way, by doing what comes naturally. It's often called "muscle memory," and some studies have supported the idea that true memory literally resides there—in the legs of dancers and in the fingers of musicians, and not just in the brain.

In the white-collar world, muscle memory is more of a metaphor, but it's just as important. When new MBAs are beginning their consulting careers at McKinsey & Company, for example, they get extensive training in how to write a presentation.[4] It's assumed that they already know how to use PowerPoint, so the training drills into them a very structured approach to making a logical argument. To keep a story flowing, every slide needs a narrative arc of situation, complication, and implication. Every slide has to have a headline that actually says something—not "Three Options for Growth" but "Best Growth Options Require Acquisitions." Since everybody in the firm gets so much training and practice early in their careers, they have an easier time writing their presentations quickly and well.

After training comes practicing, the mundane work of staying in shape. Great virtuosos work out every day, because if they didn't, they would start to lose whatever it is that makes them so good in the first place. In his study of performers and performance, the cognitive psychologist K. Anders Ericsson noted that great performers in the arts and in sports don't like practicing more than anybody else.[5] What distinguishes them is the discipline to "just do it."

Practicing also means working on a piece before putting it in front of an audience. When an orchestra is preparing a piece, even an old warhorse that the musicians know by memory, it still rehearses. Ask musicians why James Levine is such a great conductor, and most will tell you it's because of the time and focus he puts on rehearsing his orchestras. It was the main ingredient in building the Metropolitan Opera orchestra into one of the country's most renowned.

Like artists, businesspeople are obsessed with performance. To listen to managers, performance is the sine qua non of their world. Only, by *performance* they mean the measured completion of their essential tasks. And the measures are usually, but not always, expressed in numbers, such as "fourth-quarter sales increased 10 percent."

When businesses talk about the organization's performance, they use a statement of profit and growth, of

Act Three: See Your Work as a Work of Art

ROAs, ROEs, and lots of other Return Ons. Every business magazine has its lists of the top ten and bottom ten performers. With products, performance is the effective working capacity of the thing made, be it machine, toy, or garment. And with employees, a "performance review" gives feedback on how good a job the boss thinks they're doing.

How can you obsess about peak performance when you have to satisfy customers every day, keep the factory up and running, and continuously improve all the while? The answer, paradoxically, comes in focusing more on the day-to-day work. This is equivalent to the artist's practicing. It's where you work on technique and basic skills.

You can practice writing, being more exact and more vivid at the same time. You can practice listening better, being actively there and not just passively present. You can even practice reading, casting your net more broadly each day, looking for new ideas or leads or people. Practicing prepares you for those moments when you need to rise to peak performance—like each time you acquire a customer, lose a key employee, or bring a new offer to market. If you are a manager, you will need to rise to crises, people will need you. Practicing will help your performance.

One other sense of performance is undervalued in the business world, at least by comparison to the arts. This is the act of performing, of making whatever you're doing interesting and meaningful to others. Anyone who has sat through a boring presentation knows it would be far more productive if people only knew how to bring drama and presence into the room.

Imagine how much more interesting and productive business and work could be if such qualities were part of the everyday environment. The next time any of your people give a speech, especially to customers, be sure they remember that a presentation does not a performance make.

Dramatic techniques can help you reach out, motivate, and inspire leadership presence. The Ariel Group, a troupe of performers who are also consultants, tell their clients that effective leadership stems from doing four things well: being really present, reaching out to the people around you, communicating expressively, and having the authenticity that comes from self-knowledge.[6]

When you produce your work artistically, you are not just delivering it to the market—you are presenting it. You are focusing on your performance and bringing it to life with a sense of presence. And this ability to produce great performances comes from the skills of *practiced presence.*

Energy Exchange:
Create ▸ Produce ▸ **CONNECT**

Audiences can send energy back onto the stage, or not. A dancer, actor, or musician can either receive an electric charge or be stripped to pieces by the audience's lack of energy. Customers can do the same thing for or to a business. In both the arts and business, creative flow isn't a one-way street; it's an exchange of energy.

A good salesman always has more than one way of working with his customers. The style that might work for one person buying a car—playing up the horsepower and the competitive specs—might not work for somebody else who really wants a hassle-free car. Selling to an impulse purchaser takes a different set of skills than closing the deal with a price-shopper. The salesman is successful if he is able to sense what is and what isn't connecting with the customer and then instantaneously tailor his approach. In other words, if he listens to his audience.

Marketing sees a business from the customer's point of view. A customer-focused firm wants to know how to fulfill customers' needs, and that is surely a worthy purpose. Although marketing starts with customers, it only rarely sees those customers as a regular energizing source.

Whether we are referring to consumers, audiences, customers, clients, fans, or end-users, you can reach them with an artistic sensibility that sends energy back upstream in the flow. Audiences partner with performers on stage to create magic; viewers partner with artists to evoke emotion. As the old saw has it, audiences (and customers) get the performances they deserve.

A principal dancer with the San Francisco Ballet told us he did a very good show one Tuesday night. A dynamic flowed between him and the audience. The next night, Wednesday, he managed to be even more alive, but the audience didn't return as much energy. There was about a third less. He kept losing them, and he had to pull them with him more. The dancer said, over the weekend "I got to thinking, 'What's going on?' and I realized Wednesday was the last night added to the subscription mix. These people had been watching full seasons for only two years, while the Tuesday night audience had been watching ballet for much longer. They were willing to pick something up and run with it. 'All right, let's play ball.' I was picking up the little hesitation from the Wednesday night audience; they were sitting back and having a good experience but not committing to the same degree."

Both of us, Stan and David, do a lot of public speaking—itself a performing art—and here's a little method we use for gauging the audience. Very early on in a speech, in the first couple of minutes, we say something a little bit funny, not the punch line to a joke but simply a play on words. If the audience is with us from the get-go and the energy is already flowing both ways, then the line gets a laugh; we know the audience is coming along with us, and we're going to do this thing together. If they don't laugh, it's clear they're more passive or reserved. It isn't that the joke bombed but just that we're working with a different kind of audience, one that has to be won over by presenting lots of good ideas before they'll send energy back.

Another thing to listen for is "the silence." A special kind of silence results when performers know that they and the audience are perfectly attuned to one another. It's the kind where you can hear a pin drop, not the kind that says the audience's minds are elsewhere. Hume Cronyn, the actor, said, "The most magical moment in the theater is a silence so complete that you can't even hear people breathe. It means you've got them!"[7]

Listening to your audience can go a step further, to actually partnering with your customers. Meg Whitman, for example, runs eBay by letting the user community shape its strategy.[8] When her customers told her that eBay's payment system didn't work as well as PayPal's, she dumped hers and bought the better one.

In both the art and business worlds, good performers partner with their customers to produce wonderful experiences, and bad ones don't. When successful, producers and consumers, performers and audiences energize each other equally. The right approach makes passive receivers into active participants, creating a mutually reinforcing energy exchange.

The artistic processes of creating, producing, and connecting have their parallel in the economic flow. The processes in the latter are linear and quantifiable. In the artistic flow, by contrast, they are magical—but still manageable. Creativity is a process with knowable phases, and all but one are open to the rational management techniques. Only the breakthrough moment remains mysterious, better described by art than by anything as systematic as management. In the production process, new meaning can be added to familiar notions like practice and performance. The theatrical notion of "presence" is pertinent to every leader and manager. And businesses can connect with customers with the same exchange of energy as performing artists connecting with their audiences.

The processes of creating, producing, and connecting each have artistic natures expressed as dualities. The dualities—managed inspiration, practiced presence, and energy exchange—bring magic into the arts and can do the same for our work and our customers.

CHAPTER SEVEN

Find the Artistic in Everything You Do

Everything has an aesthetic and can be undertaken with artistry. Or, more precisely, everything can have an aesthetic if we choose to give it one, and that includes everything in business and in our work. We're accustomed to sensing an aesthetic when painters capture landscapes, musicians play harmonies, and actors create memorable characters. We're less used to sensing artistry when dentists fill cavities, assembly lines run perfectly, and salespeople satisfy

customers. It's there to be had in routine and useful activities, though it takes conscious effort.

Adding an aesthetic to our business activities brings elements like beauty and balance, meaning and enjoyment to them, and all business activities would benefit from such qualities. We can build artistic qualities into the work we do and the products and services we create. The more artful we make the processes, the richer are the outputs. To demonstrate this in a variety of economic contexts, we will discuss adding artistry to six different aspects of business: the value chain, marketing, technology, finance, organization, and careers.

Value Chain: From Vertical Fiefdoms to Horizontal Flows

The shift in business emphasis from vertical structure to horizontal flow is a major change over the last two decades, and with it comes a very different aesthetic.

During the industrial era, when mass was more important than motion, and scale was more important than speed, *value chain* became a standard concept. With the speed of information technology and the reengineering shift to horizontal processes, *value flow* became the preferred image. Today *chain* and *flow* are used interchangeably, which mixes metaphors—a bad aesthetic, but standard business usage nevertheless. The terms mean basically the same thing, but when you think in terms of flow, the aesthetic shifts from static to fluid, from separated to connected, from discrete to continuous, and from vertical to horizontal.

Organization charts are set up vertically around reporting relationships; value chains are set up horizontally around processes and flows from raw materials through consumption of the finished product. We now see vertical elements—strategy, production, distribution, marketing, and financial underpinnings—as part of a continuous horizontal flow, with the customer at the far end, and the creator at the front end. A firm in this flow may occupy one or several, but seldom all, places along the way. The boundaries separating the elements become less important than creating seamless links connecting them all together.

Which activities does a company need to undertake itself, and for which activities should it rely on others? Some clothing manufacturers, like Levi Strauss, have dedicated company stores as well as distribution links to retailers, websites, mail order, and so on. Retailers, like the Gap, sell clothes but usually don't make them; they rely on advertising to reach customers but pay advertising agencies and television networks to do this for them. In each case, the firm occupies key portions of its value chain but not the whole thing.

The same decisions are made in the arts. Modern dancers often choreograph their own work, but ballet dancers seldom do. Jazz frequently unites the acts of composing and performing, while classical music, at least since Rachmaninoff, seldom does so. The larger question is which business should you be in, and which should you stay out of? Ah, the aesthetic beauty in asking the right questions.

Sometimes you need to expand your coverage along the value chain. Opera America, for example, historically saw their role as an industry association that represented opera companies, not opera itself. We proposed that they adapt their strategy, that they should be "evolving to equally address improving the quality and growth of the creation, presentation, and consumption of opera." The critical word was *equally*, and the operative word was *evolving*. Like other arts associations, Opera America was formed, nurtured, and run by production companies that are understandably resistant to yielding their control, yet they also are wise enough to see the strategic advantage in focusing on the larger picture—opera rather than opera companies. Their board now includes composers, talent agents, business executives, and a volunteers' representative, with almost a third of the positions held by people not heading member companies. By evolving to equally address all three links in their value chain, Opera America can create more value for everybody concerned.

In business, the decision about where to compete would seem to be driven by where the money is. Amazingly, though, many companies don't know where in the flow they actually make money, and where they may even be losing it. Depending on an industry's competitive dynamics, for example, the activities where value is created might not be the ones where money can be made. Too many players might just be at that step, bidding the price down. The explosion of internet-related investment created enormous value for consumers, but the crowded marketplace gave investors very little return on their investment. When everybody is offering a version of the same thing, no one is going to make money doing it.

The shift from a vertical to a horizontal aesthetic led companies to compare their performance with their competitors', commonly known as benchmarking. *Benchmarking* means comparing yourself not just to your competitors but to the best in the world in each link in the chain, each step in the process, and each element in the flow. When asking who is world class at distribution, for example, you look at UPS and FedEx, not at the other people in your industry. Benchmarking fed the outsourcing bonanza during the last ten years.

A focus on process, benchmarking, and outsourcing is now a part of how business operates. In all three, the aesthetic lies in choosing where and how to add value.

Marketing: Knowing Which End to Start At

Peter Drucker, the dean of all management writing, said marketing is "the whole business seen from the point of view of its final result, that is, from the customer's point of view."[1] In the business world this approach is universally seen as true, or at least as desirable, but from the artist's point of view this is not the case at all. The artist generally begins not with the customer but with the creative inspiration and ends with the resulting work. The businessperson, by contrast, begins at the end and asks what the customer needs. This starting point has always been at the heart of the difference between artistic and economic activities, more so, even, than the distinction between for- and not-for-profit. The artist focuses on the product; the businessperson focuses on the market. Our observation is that both orientations are incomplete: you have to embrace the duality.

From Drucker's perspective, the purpose behind any

business is to have a customer. Until you have one, you're not in business, operating, alive. This is true for the arts as well, but in a way comparable to the riddle of the tree falling in the forest. Someone has to receive the produced art, to validate it. So, we're left with the question: for whom do artists create their work?

In the Middle Ages, when the great cathedrals of Europe were built, the answer was simple. All art was created *ad maiorem gloriam dei*, toward God's greater glory. Of course, this ran the risk that bad feedback could be really, really bad, but at least a person wouldn't find out for a while.

Artists today are more likely to think of their target market as themselves, their peers, and the cognoscenti. But even when artists are market-centered, too often they seek affirmation from a very narrow set of customers—their colleagues and peers. Taken to an extreme, this becomes exclusively self-referential, as seen during the last two decades: poets have been writing more and more for one another and losing relevance as a cultural force for a larger audience.

The annals of business are littered with important creations that languished for lack of an audience. Guglielmo Marconi thought the broadest application of radio would be ship-to-shore communication. Philo Farnsworth more or less invented television, but no one remembers him because he never found his market. Who were the customers he needed to find? First he needed investors who would help him bring his invention to the market. Then he needed partners to provide the programming he could show on his televisions. And finally he needed consumers to actually buy the equipment. If he had listened to his audiences, they would have told him that he had a chicken-and-egg problem. Great idea, but call me when it's ready. David Sarnoff at RCA jumped in and almost literally stole the show, because he knew how to put the necessary pieces together.

Perhaps the greatest difference between the two flows is in which end you start at, the product or the market. Great performers in both art and business bring the two perspectives together.

Technology: Making Magic Real

As science fiction writer Arthur C. Clarke put it, any sufficiently advanced technology is indistinguishable from magic.[2] And a wonderful definition of technology is, in Alan Kay's words, "what wasn't around when you were born."[3] Language, clothing, pencils . . . they're not magic, because they've been around at least as long as you have. If you're over fifty, then programming your VCR is a technological challenge. If you're over thirty, you might find it a challenge to blend multitasking and instant messaging, whereas it is totally natural for teenagers. Typically, the more established people are, the more they prefer the familiar and resist new technology. It's those who are enfranchised by its uses that embrace it.

New technology makes for new aesthetics. Before the 1930s the most popular singers were sopranos and tenors because, in a world without amplification, their voices sounded more clearly above the altos, the basses, and the orchestras accompanying them. The same was true in pop music and jazz until new technologies, such as electrical recording, the condenser microphone, and radio technology, made the baritone the dominant pop singer. Bing Crosby was the first male vocalist to master microphone technology, to take advantage of how it allowed singers to use a more natural, less stylized technique. Radio was conducive to baritones, like Crosby, with deeply nuanced voices. Most major male vocalists for the last seventy years, like Elvis Presley and Frank Sinatra, have been baritones.

Radio reinforced baseball's position as our national pastime, yet when TV came along, the team owners were terrified. They feared no one would go to the ballparks anymore, that they'd all stay home and watch the game on TV. Instead, the opposite was true. Television helped build audiences for sports, expanding the market and the industry. The movie industry has been through this cycle of fear and loathing twice—first with television and then with the

VCR. Now, digital technology, file sharing, downloading, and DVD burners are bringing on a third bout. While the Recording Industry Association of America continues to sue grandparents and teenagers alike, Felix Oberholzer-Gee and Koleman Strumpf released a study in March 2004 that showed that downloading music had no effect on CD sales.[4] In all of these cases, whether we're talking about baseball or burning CDs, each change of technology eventually advances the industry as a whole and changes the aesthetics.

Technology changes all the links in the chain, all the segments of the flow. As technology has advanced from Stone Age tools to silicon wafers, its impact has kept moving further forward in the flow and closer to the consumer. Technology's greatest impact during the shift from hunting and gathering to agriculture was in how things were created. Industrial technologies had their greatest impact on how things were produced. Today technology's greatest impact is on the way goods are distributed and consumed. Each advance in technology changed business aesthetics, the artistic flow of business, in a different way.

In our era, the first big change in the distribution aesthetic was the bar code, and the second will be the radio frequency identification (RFID) tag. The bar code was first used in 1974 at a Marsh supermarket in Troy, Ohio, to scan a package of Wrigley's chewing gum. The next generation of bar codes will exploit chips that emit radio frequencies. A nearly ubiquitous network of sensors can pick up these radio signatures, so that every coded item can be located in real time, anytime, anywhere. That includes every cereal box in the supermarket, every syringe in the hospital, every shipping container on a dock, every suitcase at an airport, and every book in the library.

The combination of bar codes and the internet has been revolutionary. Every time a laser scanner captures the code and records it, the item is connected to everyone, from producer to distributor to customer. Answers to questions like "Where is the item now?" or "When was it delivered?" become easily, cheaply, and instantly knowable. Applications of this connectivity are everywhere. The technology is universally important—it can help you locate your lost keys, and it can help fight terrorism. Every time people use their internet connection, make cell phone calls, or even show their photo IDs, they publicize their identity and location. LoJack auto antitheft devices have been popular for years; soon they'll be online. The ability to put antitheft devices on our pets and children is almost irresistible.

For better *and* for worse, the changes are nevertheless magical. We are moving toward a hyperconnected world where everything can be located everywhere all the time. Technologies like these are a mixed blessing, and they will certainly change the aesthetic of our lives. Changing technologies make magic real by changing the aesthetics and amplifying the artistic flow of business.

Finance: Balancing Efficiency and Flexibility

Finance has a reputation for being just a bean counter's profession, keeping records of what has already happened (and, more recently, for hiding activities that shouldn't have happened). But you need to know what your costs were and how much money you've made—that's what the income statement tells you. You also need to know the difference between what you own and what you owe—that's what the balance sheet is for. Together, they tell you what's been going on in your business.

If a business is absolutely predictable, you don't need to pay much attention to the finances. But in a volatile environment, good financial information makes flexibility and adaptiveness possible. You have a gas gauge in your car not to tell you how much gas you've used but how much you have left. The better gauges tell you how many miles more you can drive before you run out of fuel, and the really good ones are connected to a GPS display giving directions to the nearest gas stations. Finances change the aesthetics of business the way gas gauges change the aesthetics of travel.

Volatility is the one constant for any business. So keeping track of the finances of a business needs to be about more than just record keeping. Businesses have three approaches to managing their finances in volatile environments.

First, have a strong balance sheet, with enough cash in the bank and some unused borrowing capacity up your sleeve. This is what Joseph had the Pharaoh do, putting aside surplus from the seven prosperous years to prepare for the seven lean years. It's not a new business strategy, but it is a good one.

Second, minimize investments by not spending money until you have already made a sale. Dell Computer perfected this. When you buy a computer from Dell, you give them your credit card number, and they immediately get their money. They assemble the computer and ship it to you the following day, but they only pay for the parts that went into your computer thirty or even forty-five days later. In other words, every time they make a sale, their investment in working capital goes down! In the aesthetics of finance, that's beautiful.

The third strategy for volatile times is to own only those assets that are truly core to your needs. You might even be better off if somebody else owned assets you use every day.

Shipping and trucking companies, for example, seldom own the steel cargo containers used around the world. The containers are owned by leasing companies like Xtra and GE Capital. Similarly, GE Capital owns the engines on many aircraft, and the airlines pay only for the thrust they use, not for the metal. In other words, even when certain assets are essential to a company, it probably doesn't need to own them. Under the new financial aesthetic, possession is nine-tenths of yesterday.

If businesses didn't have to cope with volatility and uncertainty, they wouldn't need to think about finance. Their bank balances would be all the information they needed. But instead, financial officers have to prepare for uncertainty without tying up assets and reducing profits. The artistic flow of finance lies in blending and balancing efficiency and flexibility.

Organization: Changing Inside as Fast as Outside

The best insight we ever heard about organizations was from GE's Jack Welch: "When the rate of change outside exceeds the rate of change inside, the end is in sight." Is this true for most organizations? You betcha.

Act Three: See Your Work as a Work of Art

The old aesthetic was to organize for stability instead of for change. We looked for efficiencies that came from standardization. This created top-down organizations in which everybody had a boss, and the important people had many layers of people reporting to them. Hierarchies like this slow down the flow of information. It has to go up one side of the pyramid and down the other before it gets to the person who needs it.

The world outside organizations, however, moves a great deal faster. People are connected to each other through networks instead of hierarchies. Twentieth-century organizations were built around concentrating technologies; twenty-first-century organizations will be built around distributive ones. Information about opportunities moves with the speed and flexibility with which data moves on the internet. Any time a bottleneck occurs, the information finds a way to flow around it, and since information moves more quickly in a network than in a hierarchy, so does change.

AT&T had a hard time competing with Sprint, MCI, and all the Baby Bells in the 1990s because it couldn't keep up internally with the external world that deregulation was reshaping. Too many people at AT&T spent their time with other company employees instead of with customers.

To begin changing your organization's aesthetic, its mindset about what's desired, try this exercise. Draw two circles, one for your organization and one for your market, making the size of each circle proportionate to the amount of time you spend there. If you're like most people, the organization circle will be much bigger than the one for the market. Now, draw a line connecting the centers of each circle and place a mark where the center of gravity seems to be. If the mark is inside your own organization, not even meeting the market halfway, then you're in trouble.

A business is *what* you do, and an organization is *how* you do it. In this cause-and-effect relationship, the business comes first, and the organization follows; by definition, organization lags behind. Get out of this bind by shifting your focus: when confronted with an organizational problem, don't try to solve it. Focusing on the internal problem will only put you further and further behind. Instead, find the business issue that created the organizational one, and solve it. The answer to most organizational questions lies in focusing on the business out there in the marketplace. Results are outside; inside are only costs.

The aesthetic for beautiful organization comes from narrowing the gap between internal and external change as much as possible, from making sure that the firm is never too firm. You do this by opening the borders and boundaries of your organization so that internal activities are run by external marketplace rules. Capital allocation, staffing, and compensation—almost any process can be run more quickly and effectively using market rules and market prices.

In truth, real-time organization, where internal adjustments are only a nanosecond behind external changes, is still an aesthetic ideal. Realistically, if the lag at least remains constant, then management is doing a respectable job of keeping up with change. If managers reduce the lag, they're artists doing a beautiful job.

Career: Balancing Money, Mastery, and Meaning

They say that if you don't know where you're going, any road will take you there. That's how most people approach their careers. We spend untold amounts of money crafting strategies for our organizations, and then we fail to give the same attention to developing strategies for our organizations' most valuable resources—ourselves!

People take jobs for lots of reasons, and during the course of a career they take lots of jobs. While we consider many factors in all career decisions, most of them fit into three categories—money, mastery, and meaning. The aesthetic lies in knowing which one to emphasize at a given moment and how to balance different elements over the long run.

In our first jobs we often focus on learning the ropes

and mastering something—a field (medicine, sales, not-for-profits), a company (Microsoft, City Hall, the Marine Corps), a skill (teaching, software development, acting, accounting), or just entry-level basics like showing up on time, completing tasks, and getting along with coworkers. Midcareer, money may matter more, when we are faced with big-ticket items like children and mortgages. Meaning may be most salient when looking back on our accomplishments and assessing whether we made the right choices. In the long term, blend and balance is key.

Think about everybody who works in your organization. If you could know only one of these three things about each of them, which would you choose—how much they earn, what makes them skilled, or what is most meaningful to them in what they do? Chances are the dollar figures wouldn't be your first choice, or perhaps you might like to know different items for different people. Now go a step further and ask yourself, what do you think other people who work with you might answer? There's an aesthetic operating here.

The trio of money, mastery, and meaning gives you a simple framework for evaluating your choices. If you're like most people, the most important element is the one to which you tend to pay the least attention. You need all three, and ignoring one doesn't make it any more likely to develop. At times advancement in one of the elements is unavailable in the job you have. If so, then focus on the others. But sooner or later you'll need to give the neglected one its due, even if it means looking for it in a new job or even in a new career. Ignoring one of your basic needs indefinitely will lead it to atrophy, to your detriment. A career's economic flow is about only one of the three categories; the artistic flow—the aesthetic—of a career lies in balancing money, mastery, and meaning.

Enriching Economic
Processes with Artistic Flow

Our claim is that everything has an aesthetic, and we've looked at this artistic quality in a variety of business elements: the shift from vertical fiefdoms to horizontal flows in the business value chain; the perspective that technology makes magic real; the choice to start with the product or the market; the financial art of balancing efficiency and flexibility; an organization focus that has internal changes occurring in real time relative to external change; and a career perspective that balances money, mastery, and meaning.

These should all be familiar matters to practitioners of business, and you may well have dealt with many of them without ever considering your efforts artistic. Our sense is that when you do all of the above, you are enriching the economic processes with an artistic flow; you are an artist, and your work is a work of art.

An artistic perspective improves your individual work and your company's business. Still, the word *improvement* has two meanings—more successful and more moral—and they should not be confused. The artistry of Nazi film-maker Leni Riefenstahl, for example, made her work more successful, not moral. This large issue also manifests in simple daily ways. Just because you present your idea with a fantastic song and dance or a brilliant visual, the product itself is not any better, even if the business is more successful for it. Companies like Nike have been lauded for the artistry of their commercials while criticized for their corporate practices. Art and morality are not the same thing. While finding the artistic in everything you do might or might not make you any more moral, it will make you more successful.

See Your Customers as an Audience

CHAPTER EIGHT

Artistic Outputs in Business

In business, some desired outcomes are more appropriately described as artistic than economic. The four we discuss all have a dual nature, embracing and blending seeming opposites. *Beauty* gets its power from being simultaneously stimulating and calming. *Excitement* is most compelling when we get safe thrills. *Enjoyment* comes, paradoxically, from finding freshness in a familiar context. And *meaning* is strongest when we manage to personalize what's universal. In each case, the outcome's duality enhances its power.

In this chapter we will look at outputs of artistic

processes and how they enhance the value of economic goods and services. Seeing how their strength comes from the dualities underlying them, you will be in a better position to understand people's deep desires and satisfy their emotional needs. Employing these artistic outputs, you will have powerful tools for business, work, and life.

Great works of art naturally fulfill our desires for beauty, excitement, enjoyment, and meaning. These same artistic outputs can enhance the value even of ordinary products and services as much as economic outputs can. Their contribution should not be minimized, ignored, or overlooked, even when the object evoking these qualities is commonplace or utilitarian.

Millions of us, for example, carry a tiny radio transmitter on a chip on our key ring. This Mobil Speedpass is a wireless payment device that makes the chore of filling up the tank a little more enjoyable. It functions beautifully, with an ease of use that is both impressive and reassuring. The E-ZPass device affixed to our car windshield uses the same RFID technology to pay turnpike, bridge, and tunnel tolls electronically. Truthfully, the two of us confess to a tingle of excitement from this every time we avoid long toll lines of cars backed up at cash-only tollbooths. We don't think of buying gasoline and zipping through tolls as artistic experiences, but these cases, when technology makes magic real, have aesthetic as well as economic outcomes. Speedpass and E-ZPass, in other words, actually fulfill some of our more artistic desires.

Although some artists might wince, business producers and consumers actually do find (and certainly seek) some beauty, excitement, enjoyment, and meaning in products and services. Industrial design is dedicated to this proposition; so are business design and business strategy. And the design of customer experiences, whether online or in-person, succeeds or fails depending on whether it fulfills these artful desires. So let's take a closer look at them, and particularly at the duality involved in each.

Beauty: Simultaneously Stimulating and Calming

Henry Ford had little patience for his customers' aesthetic needs. "They can have it any color they want," he famously said, "as long as it's black." Ford's crosstown competitor at General Motors, Alfred P. Sloan, saw things differently. In 1927 he wrote a memo to the head of the Fisher Body division:

> To sum up, I think that the future of General Motors will be measured by the attractiveness that we put in the bodies from the standpoint of luxury of appointment, the degree

to which they please the eye, both in contour and in color scheme, also the degree to which we are able to make them different from competition.[1]

General Motors took advantage of DuPont's discovery in 1920 of the nitrocellulose lacquer that was eventually called Duco. For two significant reasons, this lacquer replaced the paints and enamels that had been used in the industry. Duco could hold three times as much pigment, making for vivid yet lower-cost colors. And it dried in eight hours instead of two weeks, removing what Sloan called "the most important remaining bottleneck in mass production."[2] The year 1927 marked the end of the Ford Model T's production run, and, not coincidentally, it saw the institutionalization of GM's "Art and Color Section." New technology had allowed a customer-conscious CEO to make attractiveness a key part of his offer. General Motors was able to respond to its customers' desire for beauty.

It wasn't hard to make a car that was prettier than the competition's, but there's an art in knowing what's going to strike people as beautiful. As anybody who has ever had a friend fall in love can tell you, beauty can be subjective. One person's aesthetic might have very little overlap with another's.

When Picasso first showed his painting *Les Demoiselles d'Avignon* in 1907, the art world didn't know what to make of it. The painting didn't look like a picture by any stretch of the imagination. It was jagged and distorted and angular. But what Picasso was doing in the picture was providing a fundamentally new answer to the basic problem of painting—how do you represent a three-dimensional world in a two-dimensional medium? The poet e. e. cummings said, "always the beautiful answer / who asks a more beautiful question." Picasso's answer was to show the subject from many different angles at the same time, and cubism was off and running. As a portrait it wasn't very accurate, but it did convey its own sense of reality. Picasso summed it up: "Art is the lie that exposes the truth."

To an earlier generation, this would have made no sense. The way Romantic poet John Keats saw things, "Beauty is truth, truth beauty,—that is all ye know on Earth and all ye need to know." Looking at a Grecian urn, Keats made an interesting assertion. He believed the art on that urn always was and always would be beautiful. It was timeless. Beauty and truth were equivalents—real, eternal, and objective.

The contemporary urn that best exemplifies timeless beauty is the Waring blender. It was introduced in 1935 and never has been improved on since. The product gets its name not from its inventor but from its investor, Fred Waring, a famous bandleader. The blender's classic design stemmed from both functional and aesthetic considerations. The cloverleaf shape of the container ensures more even blending than does any other shape, and the blender's sturdy base contains a powerful motor. But Waring's aesthetic sensibilities were responsible for the art deco design of the blender, its industrial-elegant chrome base, and its heavy glass container that lets consumers see their concoctions being blended. Form followed function, but it didn't get in the way of classic beauty.

When we describe a person as beautiful, say Gwyneth Paltrow or Mikhail Baryshnikov, we mean that they are not just pleasant to look at but arrestingly so. A flower is beautiful when it is colorful, graceful, perfectly proportioned, vivid, and fragile. The starry night sky is beautiful because of its immensity and subtlety. In all three of these cases—animal, vegetable, and mineral—underlying the beauty is a paradox, a duality. Beauty simultaneously quickens the pulse and slows us down.

The first time a friend of ours saw the Venus de Milo, it was by accident. He was racing through the Louvre, going from one must-see to another. Rounding a corner, he saw the most radiant statue, white marble almost glowing in the light coming in through windows on either side. Even before recognizing what he was looking at, he stopped in his tracks. Real beauty, like the Venus, is both stimulating and restful. We get the same sensation being served by a world-class waiter or a million-dollar lawyer: a calm comes from being taken care of by the truly competent.

This oxymoronic duality of calming stimulation explains why beauty is so memorable. Whether in a picture, an appliance, a pretty face, or a way of doing business, beauty has timelessness to it. The artist, whether a Picasso or a Sloan, finds that balance between exciting and arresting, between compelling and calming. That is the hallmark of a beautiful design.

Excitement: Safe Thrills

A character in William Finn's musical *Falsettos* sings, "I would kill for the thrill of first love." He is bored with his current romantic arrangements, and he's feeling the itch. He's going to go looking for someone new, but what he's really looking for is excitement. And what could be more exciting than first love, with the uncertainty, novelty, and risk that go with it? The first time you are in love and feeling out of control, it's scary, because you don't know where you will end up. Will you make a fool of yourself, get your feelings hurt, do stupid things, and maybe find out that someone loves you back? It's like being on a roller-coaster ride, except you don't know how long it lasts or whether you'll end up where you started. The opposite danger, of course, is the complete safety of a stable relationship that's bereft of any thrills. It's the duality that delivers the excitement.

Socially, we like challenges and stimulation at work. We care about fashion in cell phones and footwear. We brag about having eaten at fabulous, undiscovered restaurants. We are attracted to art that is edgy and provocative. We love to be first on our block at anything and to have the Joneses keeping up with us. We want to be where the buzz is, over the thrill line but still in the safe zone.

In business, producers are similarly called on to respond to our itch for excitement, curiosity, wanderlust, and such; some businesses exist almost exclusively to fill the need for excitement. Gambling in the United States is a trillion-dollar industry. You can look on gambling as a stupidity tax, but most of its customers know that the odds are against them. Gambling isn't a way to make money, it's a way to spend money. Most people who gamble do it for the excitement, for the rush; only the addicted push beyond the safe zone.

The travel industry also caters to our need for excitement. "What happens in Vegas, stays in Vegas" had been just a stock phrase until advertising executive Billy Vassiliadis heard former Secretary of Education William Bennett on a talk show discussing his well-publicized gambling losses.[3] When the all-too-human moralizer said, "I guess 'What happens here, stays here' applies to everybody but me," the ad man knew exactly how he could reach his audience. Promise them that things *happen* in Vegas, but that nobody will ever be the wiser for it. Offer them the can't-lose contradiction of safe thrills.

Judging from television commercials, automobiles are sold on that same basis. Watching cars zoom along twisting, mountainous roads is exhilarating. Seeing them crawl through congested city streets is less scenic but closer to our daily experience. The commercials play to our sense that our lives would be a little bit better, if we only had a little more sizzle in them. The fantasy is thrilling yet safe.

Excitement motivates consumers. So what motivates businesses? If you are trying to reach a business-to-business market, is excitement a useful selling proposition? Yes, because excitement isn't just a consumer's desire or an artist's desire, it's a human desire. The challenge is finding how it manifests itself in different settings.

Business executives get a lot of their thrills from competitiveness. Nothing is more exciting than beating the competition. If you are selling a product or a service that helps your customers outrun their competitors, your customers' emotional needs are as important as their purchase specs. And the way to motivate some salespeople—in addition to money, of course—is to help them feel excited. Great salespeople are hunters, not order-takers, and the thrill of the hunt is much of the fun.

People's desire for excitement ranges from safe to scary. Somewhere between the two are the challenges that stretch us but that we can rise to, the challenges that give us a sense of flow. For most people, bungee jumping just once is enough, not because they don't like it but because they only need to do it once to remember the rush. The adrenaline rush you get from succeeding in something outlandish is one that you don't quickly forget. Excitement is not an economic output, it is an artistic outcome with economic consequences.

Enjoyment: Both Fresh and Familiar

It's easier to enjoy what we are somewhat familiar with than something completely new. Broadway musicals give us all the big songs in the overture, so that when we hear them in the show we'll feel a subconscious warmth of recognition. Humor is enjoyable because it connects the familiar with the unexpected. Before they were replaced by "reality" shows, television sitcoms were a form of cultural comfort food. Knowing the characters and the contexts made shows like *M*A*S*H* and *Friends* a safe, reliable part of our entertainment diet.

Artistic Outputs in Business

Businesses satisfy their customers' desires for the enjoyable by bringing fresh approaches to familiar situations. Jet-Blue, for example, has achieved tremendous customer loyalty by making their travel not only cheap but also enjoyable. Everybody gets an all-leather seat, and their in-flight entertainment is the best in the industry. Where Southwest Airlines provides entertainment from some-times-funny flight attendants hamming it up on an open mike, JetBlue provides twenty-four channels of satellite TV. Back on the ground, JetBlue is just as enjoyable to deal with. Call the 800 number, and you talk to someone who sounds like a real person, not a drone who isn't allowed to say anything that's not in the customer care software script. Even the online experience—clean, clear, and quick—is enjoyable.

Companies sometimes provide enjoyment in their name and branding. In a Boston suburb, Death Wish Piano Movers has an unforgettable aesthetic that brings a smile to your face. Each of its shiny black trucks has the skull and cross-bones painted on the side, and all the employees dress in black. In the PC repair business, a tongue-in-cheek aesthetic is almost de rigueur. Geeks on Call, Geeks on Time, and Geeks Online, among others, are happy to play up to stereotypes just to make doing business with them a little less stressful and a little more enjoyable. You see the same aesthetic at work in all the . . . *for Dummies* books.

Act Four: See Your Customers as an Audience

Hospitals strike a lot of people as frightening and unpleasant, not as a place to enjoy. Some specialty hospitals, though, like the New England Baptist, make inpatient and outpatient surgery more pleasant by ensuring the entire process runs smoothly from the patient's point of view. Instead of employing the hurry-up-and-wait mentality that the army perfected and most hospitals adopted, they make the patient feel well taken care of. They provide more continuity of care and fewer encounters with doctors and nurses whom the patient has never met. Because the hospital specializes in a few kinds of surgeries, it can provide the efficiencies of an assembly line without the factory-floor feeling. The Baptist is unexpectedly refreshing, and it's no wonder that AARP named them one of the ten best places for knee and hip orthopedic care.

Enjoyment, like surgeries, can run the gamut of intensities. We enjoy seeing a cartoon that makes us smile, even if we forget it a minute later. We enjoy doing a crossword puzzle, feeling satisfaction tinged with competitiveness. At its deepest level, enjoyment is ecstatic, taking us out of the normal flow of our lives and filling us with joy. The very word *joy* is such a strong one that it is rarely used unless we're talking about sex, religion, or our children. But there's no reason why we can't find joy in other parts of our lives.

Artistic Outputs in Business

We all can get as much joy from our work as from recreation. When we are absorbed, concentrating and focused on getting something done, we are experiencing the flow that brings enjoyment. Ria Kittay, a piano tuner, told us, "If you find something that you love to do, you'll never have to work a day in your life. That's what I did, and I've always been happy about it." She does the same work every day but can always find the freshness in the challenges she faces.

At the same time, we have to do lots of jobs that no one likes doing. That's why it's called *work*. Drudge work, where it's harder to find the joy and the aesthetic, will always exist, but doing it gives you the opportunity to create work that is meaningful and satisfying.

From what makes us laugh to what leaves us satisfied is this common thread: enjoyment comes from finding what's fresh in what's familiar. The context of familiarity makes it safer to be open to new experiences. And unexpectedness can be a pleasant surprise, whether it's in the form of a joke or a first-rate customer experience. Enjoyment is an artistic output satisfied by the duality of familiar freshness.

Meaning: Personalize
What Is Universal

Meaning comes from the conversation between the specific and the general. One type of meaning is about context: "What is this information really telling me?" Another, related type of meaning is about significance and purpose: "Where do I find meaning in my life?" In both, meaning gets its punch from establishing the connection between the personal and the universal.

To find the meaning in a piece of art, you have to look at it in the context of other art. In dance, in music, and in literature, much of what happens is a comment on what has gone before. In painting, the century of modernism has been predominantly about ideas and not about beauty. A gallery owner told a novice art buyer on *Queer Eye for the Straight Guy* that when buying contemporary art, you shouldn't just look for beauty, you should look for meaning. Look for what the artist is telling you he or she is thinking about. The same goes for picking a retirement fund. Before you trust your future to the fund managers at Fidelity or Charles Schwab, it pays to find out how what they're thinking about the market in general relates to your needs specifically. What meaning have they been gleaning from the market's ups and downs, and how are they positioning their funds in a way that will benefit you?

Smart customers want to understand the meaning in the goods or services they're thinking of buying. For example, someone buying a piece of furniture sooner or later is going to ask something like "Why does this chair cost so much?" The salesman might then answer, "It's because of the quality of the construction, the hand-tied springs, the dove-tailed joints, and the kiln-dried hardwood frame." "The what?" "Okay, let's talk for a moment about what you are buying when you buy a good piece of furniture." Good customers want the context, whether they know it at first or not. They might even want to understand the vendor's objectives and business model. What percentage of your business, they might ask, comes from repeat customers? Does the larger part of your margin come from sales or service? Are the salespeople on salary or commission? These questions are a way of making sense of the specifics of an offer in comparison to others.

The other type of meaning, which we all look for, is personal meaning. On Maslow's hierarchy of needs, the search for meaning comes after basics like eating and sleeping, but it's still a fundamental need that everybody has. As long as a person has the basics covered, then meaning is a need he or she can't help thinking about from time to time. "Why am I here? What am I accomplishing? What will I leave behind?" When we think about what gives our life meaning, we think in both the present and the future tense. "What have I created, and what will I leave behind?"

Billy Crystal, the actor-comedian, tells the story of something he learned early in his career. He came off stage thinking he had been terrific, only to have a mentor tell him, "You didn't leave something." To be successful on stage, Crystal explains, you must leave something of yourself for the audience, something that lets them know you, who you are, what you are as a person, not just as a performer. He says that since then, when he performs he always leaves something of himself for his audience. The message is: let people see the person behind the lines.

We all pursue success and meaning during our lives, but it's hard to do both at the same time. It's easier to postpone one or the other, to try to sequence them somehow. The altruist says, "I'm going to do socially relevant work now while I'm young, before I have to settle down and start providing for a family." The pragmatist proposes doing things in the opposite order. "I'm going to make my first million by the time I'm thirty-five, and then I'll have the freedom to do the charitable stuff." Ebenezer Scrooge was like this, until he got his wake-up call.

In 1983, Steve Jobs made an offer to the president of Pepsi–Cola, John Sculley. The revolution in PCs was taking off, and Jobs wanted Sculley to take over his job as Apple's CEO. In the end, Sculley's decision whether or not to take the job hinged on one question that Jobs put to him: "Do you want to spend the rest of your life selling sugared water or do you want a chance to change the world?"[4] If Sculley took the job at Apple, his work would affect literally billions of people. He would have something substantial to point to when he retired, Jobs implied. But if he stuck with his job selling soft drinks, it would be harder to see how his individual efforts had left any mark.

When Sculley made his decision to go with Apple, it wasn't about money, it was about meaning. It was about connecting personal skills to universal needs. It was about finding personal reward from helping others. As it turned out Sculley didn't last that long at Apple, but he left his mark. Without him, Apple might never have introduced the first PDA, the Newton, which in turn led the way for the Palm Pilot that is ubiquitous today.

No contemporary writer has written more effectively about the importance of meaning in work than Studs Terkel. His 1972 book, *Working*, was an oral history compiled from hundreds of interviews with people in various lines of work.[5] He talked to nurses, construction workers, waitresses, parking lot attendants, housewives, retirees, all sorts of people. Terkel's stories captured the dignity that people found in their work. People want to be good at what they do, and they want to find the flow in their work.

Several years after it was published, *Working* became a Broadway musical, with songs by Stephen Schwartz, Mary Rodgers, Craig Carnelia, and James Taylor, among others. In the finale, all the people who work in an office building, and all the people who helped build it, point out what they have done, what their contributions were. In unison they sing, "Everyone should have something to point to, something to be proud of ..."

Every time either of us starts a new project where people are working for us, that line sings in our heads. If you want people to be motivated, they have to have something to point to when their work is done. We all need something to be proud of. Artists in the studio or the sandwich shop are motivated by the need to do something well and to be recognized for their hard work and accomplishment.

Stan had a slate walkway put in at his front door, and it was laid by Ned Delacata, a very noble-looking Italian artisan with a name that sounds like notes on a musical scale. De-la-ca-ta. When it was finished, he looked at it and said, "You know, that's my little piece of posterity, the mark of my work that I'll leave behind."

Working is so effective because it uses individual stories to convey a universal theme. The need for meaning is universal; understanding what it feels like to be a schoolteacher or a stonemason gives you the particulars. The best way to affect people deeply is to share something personal. When we're in the service of a goal that is bigger than ourselves—whether it's charitable or corporate—we find what's personally meaningful. There are three different types of stonemasons. Ask one what he's doing, and he'll say he's cutting a stone. Ask another, and he'll say he's making a wall. Ask a third, and he'll say he's building a cathedral. This is about artistry, not economics.

Meaning lies in the duality of personal and universal. The meaning in a piece of art or a piece of work comes from how that thing connects to everything around it. To understand the specific, you have to understand the general. And meaning in people's lives comes from the times they go outside themselves to do something for others. Whether you're talking about an artwork or a job, when something touches both the personal and the universal, it starts being meaningful.

Outputs: Satisfying Our Desires

Not every business satisfies every artistic desire in equal amounts, although it's impossible to be successful without satisfying some of them. But a few businesses have such a perfect business model that they do fire on every cylinder.

Act Four: See Your Customers as an Audience

Netflix, the online DVD rental service, is, besides Google, the only great internet business to spring up in the wake of the dot-com crash. If you combined Amazon.com with a video store and your public library, you'd get something like Netflix. Here's how it works. After setting up your account and giving them your credit card information, you go online and list all the movies you want to see. Netflix mails the DVDs to you, and you can keep up to three at a time. Whenever you return a DVD in their pre-paid, pre-addressed envelope, they mail you the next DVD on your list. You get a confirmation e-mail every time they mail you a disk or get one back. Netflix makes the whole rental experience not only faster but cheaper. It costs twenty dollars a month—less than just the late fees many of us pay on rentals from the video store.

Netflix does a superb job of satisfying customers' desires. They offer the safe thrills or excitements, letting you constantly try out new videos in a no-risk, no-variable-cost way. It's enjoyable—they continually send new videos to you, but in a familiar, friendly way. It can even be meaningful, giving us a chance to personalize our entertainment to a degree that's never been possible before, connecting us with other people we'll never meet, people who made, reviewed, watched, and were touched by the movies and TV reruns we find ourselves watching. What's really beautiful is their way of doing business. While it may seem antisocial, it's so seamlessly simple that it's almost a prescription to relax and feel taken care of.

Wonderful businesses have the traits of wonderful artwork. They provide the same outputs of beauty, excitement, and the like. Each artistic output gets its power from connecting two sides of a duality. If you can create goods and services that meet people's needs for stimulating calm, for safe excitement, for fresh familiarity, and for personalizing the universal, you'll create the customer satisfaction that runs deep and lasts long. In other words, delivering the artistic outputs customers are really looking for will give you the chance to create something that is both meaningful and valuable.

CHAPTER NINE

Do Your Customers Send You Energy?

Business flows from inputs, through processes, to outputs. In the magic of metaphors, it also loops back. When the entire flow works optimally, customers are more than passive receivers of outputs; as we said earlier, they also send energy back up the flow to providers. Customers energize well-run businesses regularly.

The clothing designer who gets his ideas from trend-setting teenagers, the fast-food chain that responds to customers' desires for healthier fare, and the accounting firm

Do Your Customers Send You Energy?

that honors their obligations to the investment community and not just their clients—these are examples of businesses energized by their true and ultimate customers.

In this chapter, we look at a few industries that produce their best work when they get their energy from their customers. Architecture and interior design are fields that blend artistic and economic flow in almost everything they do. When they do it right, both artistic and economic flows send energy back from customers up to the providers. Sometimes it happens, and other times not. In music, symphony orchestras and opera companies attract many of the same listeners, but opera companies have found it easier to evolve and connect to their still-growing audiences. As they become more responsive to their customers' needs for artistic outputs like beauty and enjoyment, these fields will do a better job at creating meaning that will outlive them and their customers.

When energy isn't flowing between the provider and the customer, something is wrong. Usually, it doesn't mean that customers aren't sending back energy; it means that the provider isn't paying attention. Instead it's probably using resources to fulfill its own desires more than its customers'. And when the energy flows move both ways, they reinforce one another, and the rewards increase for everyone.

Architecture and Interior Design

Architecture is the most visible of all the arts. A bad piece of music usually disappears after its first performance. A dreadful painting goes into storage. But a building is forever, at least until it is torn down. The public has to live with what architecture produces, like it or not.

Interior design is not as permanent as a building's external architecture. We expect the inside of a building to reflect the changing tastes and needs of the current occupants. One rule of thumb has it that the construction cost of a building represents only about 20 percent of what is spent over time.[1] Forty percent goes to maintaining the infrastructure like roofs and furnaces, and 40 percent goes to interior layout and furnishings. Twice as much is spent on designers' work inside the building as on what the architects did with the building in the first place.

As a profession, architecture has always had something of a split personality. Is it more like art or engineering? Is it about building things or designing them? In nineteenth-century France, the construction field was divided academically between the École des Beaux Arts and the École des Ponts et Chaussées (the engineering school). The construction of roads and bridges was given to the school of engineering, but building construction was in the school of fine arts.

This split continued in the United States. When the first Department of Architecture in the country opened at MIT in 1865, it was located not in Engineering but in the Humanities Department. As is the case at most schools, department chairmen and teachers have tended to be historians of architecture, not practitioners or engineers. And, in a pattern not unknown in other fields, academics were slower than practitioners to incorporate new technology like CAD/CAM software. By contrast to France and the United States, architecture schools in Britain and Germany locate architecture within engineering departments. As a result, architects there have often moved more quickly toward using new technological developments.

The separations between theory and practice, humanities and engineering, art and economics have long histories, maybe even going back to the pyramids. One of the many ways these separations manifest today is the never ending debate about which is more important, design or function. This debate often plays out in the conflicting approaches of exterior architects versus interior architects and designers.

Should they begin with what the client wants or with a creative response to what they think the space calls for? If you think that functionality is what really matters, then you start with that and build a design aesthetic around it. If you begin with a creative design idea, as did the architect for Sydney Opera House, you fit the functionality into the design. Both approaches require energy, experience, and imagination. But the first approach takes more energy and input from the end-user.

It gets complicated when a client is working with both types of architect/designer at the same time. A wealthy entrepreneur we know was building a seaside vacation home. Following the advice of everyone he asked, he used an architect for the exterior and a designer for the interior of his sumptuous getaway. The two planners locked horns at almost every turn. A characteristic battle involved a window area the exterior architect had designed for a vaulted room with an ocean view. The designer wanted to put window seats there for people to use while enjoying the view; the architect said that would break the visual lines of window and ocean and the furniture could be only in the middle of the room. One wanted to admire the space, the other wanted to use it. Neither thought they were slighting the aesthetic results. Ultimately, the customer decided.

The tension between design and function, of course, is moot when architects and designers take both perspectives into account. Then all start from the same premise: listening to the client. The difference is in how much weight they give to the client's voice in what they actually come up with. The ideal is a perfect balance between design and function, between aesthetics and utility, between artistic and economic flows. On the provider end, the truth about this balance lies in degrees of emphasis. On the consumer end, the truth lies less in the critics' reviews than in how the end–user feels about living or working in the finished building.

It's a question of how much energy you choose to get from your audience/customer. Sometimes architects or designers will listen to the client and use what they hear as their starting point, but they don't let it interfere with what their outcome is going to be. They spend more energy trying to turn the client around to embrace a concept they've come up with than finding ways to work with the client's creative vision.

Others take the opposite approach, which is more driven by the artistic flow. One designer we know, trained as an interior architect, explains her philosophy.

My premise is that the client is creative, whether they believe it or not. When clients say they're not creative and don't know what they want, I don't believe it. Everybody has an innate aesthetic, and it's up to me to pull it out of them.

When I start a job, for example, I'll give them dozens of magazines and packages of both green and red Post-its. I tell them to go through the pages and stick green tabs on anything that appeals to them. They don't have to know or say what or why, just stick it, and stick red tabs on what doesn't appeal to them. When I lay the pages out on the floor, I find the innate sense of what they like and don't like. Some like loud colors, some soft; some like clutter, some like order; and so on. All of it is part of their innate creativity. That's how I begin a job. And you have to key off your clients like that throughout the project, so that they're never caught short by an unexpected outcome.

Most businesses start at the end, with the customers and what they want. The arts more frequently start at the other end, with the creative concept. Good architects and interior designers strive to marry the two, starting with the customers and working on a design aesthetic that will please them. The art of business is to blend the artistic flow into the economic one, going from creative and imaginative inputs to beautiful and meaningful outputs. The economic payoff from doing this right is significant.

Even though most architects are underemployed and (they feel) underpaid, they work on only a fraction of the projects that they could. According to the National Association of Home Builders, roughly 1.3 million new single-family homes were built in the United States in 2002 alone. That same year, homeowners spent $173 billion remodeling their homes—up 10 percent from 2001—but only about 14 percent of that work involved an architect or designer.

One reason for this low rate of involvement is that hiring these professionals adds to the costs. "Most architects calculate their fees as a percentage of construction costs—usually 12 to 15 percent," notes *Architecture* magazine editor-at-large Bradford McKee.[2] And interior designers add about 15 to 18 percent. When those kinds of costs get tacked on, clients want to see results they can relate to aesthetically. Hiring these professionals adds to the cost, but the more the professionals listen to their customers, the more willingly the customers will pay.

Because the interiors of buildings are closer, literally, to the clients who dwell or work there, interior designers often have to work more closely with the customer's point of view about beauty and enjoyment. The debate is most acute when it involves public buildings and commercial spaces.

Discussions of beauty and meaning, for example, have been tantamount in deciding on the appropriate designs for the post-9/11 World Trade Center site. The challenge is to balance meaningful aesthetics and acceptable costs. If ever there was a case for blending the artistic and economic flows, this is it.

The romantic notion of an architect, embodied in Frank

Lloyd Wright, is of a visionary genius who must overcome the shackles put on him by narrow-minded clients and overdefined assignments. Just think what he could accomplish if he could only build what he imagines! This stereotype doesn't reflect the fact that most architects, famous or obscure, have done their best work when engaged with active clients with opinions of their own. The give and take of ideas and energy is responsible for successful, workable, enjoyable spaces.

Orchestras and Operas

Every field has an artistic flow from inputs to outputs and should also have a flow of energy from customers back to providers. Some performing arts have been better than others at tapping into that backflow.

Both symphonies and operas are musical art forms, related but distinct. The companies often play music by the same composers and attract similar customers. Yet the orchestral field has been in crisis for a long time, while opera companies fare relatively well.

Between 1982 and 2002, the audience for live performances of classical music in the United States—symphonies, choral music, and chamber music—grew by about 12 percent, well below the population growth of 26 percent. At the same time, the audience for opera grew by

46 percent. Part of this is due to a difference in circumstances, but part of it is due to a difference in approach. It's not that one field is better than the other, but looking at them tells us more about how to partner with audience/customers.

The malaise among orchestras may have complicated roots, but it can be seen in ephemera and in trivia, like what the audience wears, how old they are, and whether they sit quietly or react boisterously. These minutiae tell us a good deal about how well an art form is faring, whether it is winning or losing fans, whether the customers get beauty, excitement, enjoyment, and meaning for their ticket price, and whether it is connecting or disconnecting with the larger social panorama of the time.

From the time of Mozart through the Gilded Age of New York City in the early 1900s, audience and musicians were very formally dressed. At the beginning of the twentieth century, white tie and tails were commonly worn to concerts. Through the decades, audiences democratized, and those who could not afford formal wear wore their best suits and dresses instead; the musicians still dressed formally. By the end of the century, audience wear had become more and more informal, while on stage tuxedos and gowns held fast.

The widening sartorial split became comically apparent at a concert at Tanglewood in the Berkshires in Massachusetts. A visiting European orchestra played, dressed in formal black; the audience—many of whom were on summer vacation or even camping—was in tennis shoes and sandals, khakis and jeans. Ironically, the musicians were between twenty and fifty years old while the audience was mainly between fifty and eighty. So much for the casualness of youth and the formality of elders. Then, as frequently happens in summer concerts, a few people applauded between movements. The majority winced at the gaucherie, and the clappers quickly faltered and got educated about how to be "appropriately" silent and respectful until the end. The concert was grand, but the concert-going culture was all wrong-headed. Every time the customers sent energy back to the performers, they were punished.

No wonder orchestras are losing their audiences. Of course, the quality of the music and of the musicians is more important than how people dress. But the details are telling of the gap that's grown between artists and audiences in classical music. The orchestras are not following the increasing informality of their fans, they're losing their audience to age, and they're cutting off the energizing link by squelching feedback. The small things add up to a malaise from which the field suffers. Orchestras are not listening to and communicating with their audiences on small but telling matters.

Do Your Customers Send You Energy?

These things are extrinsic to artistic integrity but intrinsic to the message about relationships, and they're sending the wrong message. Would the same orchestra be less well received if the members all wore white shirts and blouses? Not at all. Would concertos be less enjoyable if audiences were allowed to shout "Bravo!" after brilliant cadenzas, the way they do after brilliant arias at operas? Are encores appreciated less when performers tell the audience what they are about to play for an encore? Is the art compromised because it is more entertaining? Vital connections between artists and audiences are about more than just the music and the words; they're also about the little things, the human connections.

Even after jazz migrated from the clubs to the concert halls, there is still a moment in every concert when the leader introduces all of the performers—whether they are a small group or a big band—to the audience. You never get that in a classical concert. Imagine the first violin introducing the other members of the string quartet to the audience, "And this is Carl Jones on viola." This would enable the audience to know who the players are as people, relate to them, acknowledge them, and create a relationship with them. Not doing so is equivalent to not introducing someone at a social gathering.

An audience's applause signals two things: customers are communicating their appreciation to performers, and they are expressing their emotions about what was performed. Discouraging clapping and verbal expression until the very end of the piece prevents consumers from expressing their emotions about what they've just seen and heard. It is like presenting a comedy and having the audience hold their laughter until the end. That would be funny—not funny-ha-ha, just funny-strange.

Both opera companies and symphony orchestras have their strengths and weaknesses, and we don't want to disparage one field and shout only bravos to the other. After all, Texaco did drop its Metropolitan Opera broadcasts after sixty-four years because there just weren't enough listeners to justify the expense. But the ways in which opera has adjusted to remain relevant to its audience hold valid lessons.

Operas have the advantage of being staged; opera companies talk about multimedia art for a multimedia age. Directors often change the time and place of an opera's setting to speak to a contemporary audience. Peter Sellars, for example, noting that murder and rape enter into the very first minutes of Mozart's *Don Giovanni*, set the opera in a South Bronx ghetto to convey the harsh circumstances. Shakespeare's plays are regularly updated in their staging, which the Bard himself did with the stories he worked with. These adjustments are clearly nods to making better connections with the audience without violating artistic integrity.

Do Your Customers Send You Energy?

Perhaps the biggest factor in opera's growth in the last twenty years is the adoption of surtitles scrolled high above the stage or on the back of the seat in front of you. We have subtitles for foreign films, so why shouldn't we have them for operas sung in foreign languages or unintelligible English? For a comedy like *The Barber of Seville*, it's wonderful to be in an audience that's laughing at the punch lines, the way audiences did when the operas were first performed. Real-time translation embodies all the artistic outputs we've emphasized. When audiences understand what's going on, operas are more beautiful, enjoyable, exciting, and meaningful. When you find ways to connect artistically with your customers, you energize your business.

This isn't complicated stuff. The message is simply that customers will respond energetically when you fulfill their desires for artistic outputs—beauty, excitement, enjoyment, and meaning. It doesn't matter whether your business is orchestras, operas, ovens, or oscillators; customers will send you energy when you pay attention to their aesthetic and artistic needs.

Improv

We close on an improvisational note. Improv, or improvisational theater, shows in microcosm all the elements of artistic flow we've described. All the inputs of imagination, emotion, intelligence, and experience are put to work. All the creative phases are packed into a managed inspiration, a delightful, unpredictable little gem. While extemporaneous, it requires enormous practice and presence to pull off, and improv often calls forth enormous energy from an audience. Anyone who has ever been to improv has experienced its enjoyment and excitement.

Improv offers excellent lessons to use in your business. A slight problem, however, is that improvisation is not a highly regarded behavior in business. It smacks of being ill prepared and sloppy. As an art form it is anything but. In jazz, in theater, and certainly in comedy, improvisation is built on a shared understanding of structures and ground rules. Many of the ground rules for improv are as valuable in the business world as in the arts.

In terms of time, improv is all present tense. The focus is on "being in the moment." If you've ever spoken with someone whose mind seemed to be elsewhere, you know they're not living in the moment. The human potential movement said, "Be here, now," and while that was a great mantra, it never quite taught how to do so on a sustained basis. Improv does teach you how.

Charna Halpern and Del Close taught improv to John Belushi, Bill Murray, John Candy, Gilda Radner, Chris Farley, Mike Myers, and many others. They teach that you don't prepare a scene, you prepare to be ready for a scene.

"A scene," according to them, "is never about what the player thinks it is going to be," so you have to be acutely present in what it is at that moment.[3]

Improv, like Japanese management, has a cardinal rule: the best way to look good is by making those around you look good. In terms of space, the focus is the group, not the individual. Grabbing onto a supporting role rather than onto the lead, for example, can be the pivot that makes a scene work, and it's a decision that has to be made in the spur of the moment.

A corollary rule, derived from the primacy of the group, is the rule of agreement: everything is "Yes, and . . ." It is never ever "No" or "But . . ." Like riding a bicycle, keeping your balance comes from forward momentum, not from stepping on the brakes. So nothing is ever wrong, there are no mistakes, and the truth will emerge by moving forward.

A common way to start an improv is for people to take turns calling out words and phrases. After a while, the group starts to search for common threads, and the words emerge into an unplanned pattern. As soon as the pattern appears, you have your theme and scene, and the improv begins midstream.

Improv is like ping-pong, not chess. The key is in spontaneity, not in thinking ahead. You have to adapt to a scene, moment by moment, following it rather than trying to control it. It has more in common with the "adapt and evolve" management model of the future than with the "command and control" management model of the past. As business embraces an adaptive mind-set, improv is becoming more at home.

Business already uses improv when people get started on a problem by "brainstorming" for a while. Ideas are offered up in quick succession, and none are evaluated or examined. Ideas first, analysis later. There aren't any bad ideas, just ones that don't end up getting used.

In 2003, the Second City comedy troupe's communications unit led more than three hundred communication workshops with revenues approaching $4 million.[4] For businesses that want to build effective work groups and foster cooperative teams, improv is an excellent vehicle. It's safer, less expensive, and more convenient than whitewater rafting or any of the typical team-building exercises. It teaches how to be committed to what you are doing, how to stay focused, how to further ideas, how to be a commanding presence, and how to deliver outstanding performance. Because it's fun, it also builds a common sense of belonging. It requires nothing more than a room and an instructor, so it's totally cheap. And you can make your first improv about an Outward Bound ropes course for executive trainees, but now we're planning ahead.

Flowing Both Ways

Improv, whether on stage or in the conference room, is about flow—in both senses. It's about being in the flow of the moment, and it's about the artistic flow of transforming inputs like imagination and emotion into outputs like enjoyment and excitement.

When you're delivering artistic outputs, remember that beauty (and enjoyment and excitement and meaning) is in the eye of the beholder. The way to know if you're providing your customers with something valuable is to look for the connection. When you're producing artistic flow, as much energy will be flowing back to you from your customer/audience as you're sending their way.

Listening to your customers, whether an architectural client or the audience in a comedy club, does more than let you know how you're doing. It takes their energy and adds it to what you are already working with; it lets you draw on their imagination, experience, and emotions as you fashion the outputs they want. When the energy goes both ways between the producer/artist and the customer/audience, the result is like an electric flow.

Throughout this book, we have talked about artistic flow and the impact it can have on your business, work, and life. Now we offer you some practical, concrete steps to harness that flow.

We've organized them around the three principal elements of the flow—inputs, process, and outputs. Half of the actions have a business and organization focus, and the other half are for you as an individual.

Input: Imagination

Business: Pick a real business problem you are facing, then come up with a list of ten diverse and famous people. Use your imagination to think what they would do to solve your problem if they were advising your company. Craft a one-sentence response from each person. The purpose is not to be cute or clever but to give you new perspectives on the problem. Here's one possible list of problem-solvers —Thomas Edison, Dilbert, Abraham Lincoln, Buddha, Arnold Schwarzenegger, Jane Austen, Michael Dell, Oprah Winfrey, Walt Whitman, and George Carlin.

Individual: If you're a reader, and by this point we assume

you are, spend as much time reading fiction as you do books on business, history, politics, or human potential. It takes real imagination to understand what makes a character who he or she is. You can get insights from Leo Tolstoy as well as from Peter Drucker, from John Irving as well as from Tom Peters. And in your business reading, do as much outside your specialty as within it.

Input: Emotion

Business: Analyze the content of your corporate vision to find the emotional juice. Depending on what you have access to, take the executive summary of your strategic plan or an important company memo. Read it with a yellow highlighter in hand, calling out the places where success depends on making an emotional connection with customers or employees. If you can read the whole document without taking the cap off the highlighter pen, you have some real work to do to give the document some life.

Individual: Take a look at your job description and your most recent performance review. What emotional qualities are included? Is it possible to succeed in your job without being able to anticipate how you will touch other people emotionally? Probably not. Circle the performance objectives that particularly require an understanding of how other people will react to what you do, and give yourself a grade on your emotional performance.

Input: Intelligence

Business: Conduct an intelligence audit of your work group to find out if you have strengths in all the types of intelligence—verbal, spatial, interpersonal, and so forth. The HR department can help you evaluate some of these capabilities, but you'll need to use your own judgment for the spatial, musical, and kinesthetic intelligences. A team with strength in every dimension will bring a more balanced and customer-focused sensibility to your offering.

Individual: Give yourself a personal intelligence audit as well, so you know whether some of your intelligences overshadow the others. Then, with the facts in front of you, think whether you are better off being a specialist or a generalist. If you hope to get by on the strength of one or two types of intelligence, make sure that matches up with your current job. Or, if your satisfaction depends on drawing more evenly on all your abilities, make sure you've found a role that lets you do that.

Input: Experience

Business: The artistic experience curve describes the relationship between experience and creativity. The longer your company has been around, the more experience it should be able to take advantage of; the more connections you've got, the more creativity you can support. Look at measures of creativity for your company, like patents per capita per year and percentage of revenues from products and services less than five years old. Are the numbers going up, in line with increasing artistic experience? If they're not, you need to take better advantage of under-utilized artistic resources.

Individual: Everybody has a back-story: how you came to be where you are now, what your motivations are, what makes you unique, and so on. When you share your experience with the people with whom you work, you'll enjoy and appreciate each other more. This is true for employees, customers, suppliers, distributors, competitors, regulators, and investors. Imagine if every card in your Rolodex had a notation or two listing that person's story.

Process: Create

Business: Four of the five steps needed to create (everything except *Click!*) are manageable processes. Pull out the project plan for one of your big business initiatives for this year. What percentage of the project timeline and budget is devoted to the steps of hunch, simmer, immerse, and verify? If it's less than 50 percent, you're probably guilty of "shoot, ready, aim," jumping right in to execute second-rate solutions instead of finding creative breakthroughs.

Individual: Even if it has been years since you've kept

a diary, start carrying a notebook—paper or electronic. Every time you see something that makes you think or laugh, jot it down. When everyone wonders where you get all your creative ideas, tell them what Yogi Berra said: "You can observe a lot by watching."

Process: Produce

Business: Here's a team-building exercise that can produce results. Give each team six square index cards, and ask them to build a cube with the cards in three minutes or less. After they've done it once, ask them if they think they could do it better next time. And then let them. In fact, have them build the cube six times; practicing something helps you do it better.

Individual: Once a week go to your sent e-mail file, choose a short one, and rework it until it reads so artfully that the recipient would notice and say, "I wish I'd said that." Keep at it until somebody says that to you about one of your actual e-mails. It will benefit both your technique and your self-confidence.

Process: Connect

Business: Bring your customers to speak at your weekly staff meetings and not just at your annual sales conference.

Whether you make mainframes, Mars Bars, or mergers, you connect with both your audience and your customers better when you get the energy flowing both ways.

Individual: You shouldn't teach more than your students can learn, and you shouldn't produce more than can be consumed. To the same point, you can't hear the audience laughing if you don't stop talking. As E. M. Forster wrote in his novel *Howards End*, "only connect." When you're at the podium, let the audience know they're doing as much work as you are. Whether on stage, in a meeting, or at the water cooler, watch for body language and nonverbal cues. Are people nodding in agreement or nodding off to sleep? What you hear your audience telling you is as important as what you are telling them.

Output: Beauty

Business: You can't benchmark beauty, since it's in the eye of the beholder, but you can use it to help you find some best practices. Take your most beautiful product or service offering, and systematically compare it with one that's not as beautiful. What can you learn from the beautiful offerings that you could apply to all your other offerings?

Individual: Make your workspace a haven of the calming stimulation that exemplifies beauty. You spend more hours a day there than you do in your living room, but you probably haven't put as much thought into how it looks. Is there something beautiful to look at, besides the pictures of your children? Create a visual focal point other than the pile of papers on the side of your desk. At the same time, make sure your workspace has a sense of energy that says "Important things get done here."

Output: Excitement

Business: Here's how to create a risk-analysis grid to help you sort out excitement from what's senseless. First, make an extensive list of decisions you face at work, such as a new product launch, outsourcing customer support, and corporate renaming. Next, create a grid where the horizontal axis shows the adrenaline level, going from boring on the left to thrilling on the right, and the vertical axis shows the risk factor, with dangerous on the bottom and safe on top. Array all the decisions on the grid. Everything in the upper right (safe thrills) should be exciting because they're desirable risks. Stay away from everything in the lower left (boring and dangerous) because they're unacceptable risks. The diagonal middle (safe and boring to dangerous and thrilling) represents varying degrees of manageable risks.

Individual: The same risk-analysis framework works just as well for managing excitement in your personal life. Use it to array the personal decisions you face, such as getting an MBA, working for a brilliant but demanding boss, and changing cities to advance your career. Find the no-brainers that are both safe and thrilling, avoid the boring and dangerous, and make informed choices about the others.

Output: Enjoyment

Business: When you're compiling your customer satisfaction surveys—a longtime business basic—add one question that goes beyond satisfaction to ask about real enjoyment. Something along the lines of "Did we do something this year that made you smile?" or "Did you enjoy using our product/service?" or "Did we do anything that made you enjoy being one of our customers?"

Individual: The next time you're in another city on business, add some time into your trip for enjoyment. Go to a park or museum, catch up with an old friend, or, better still, combine the two. You'll find that some of the meetings where your best work gets done take place outside the office, surrounded by beautiful things.

Output: Meaning

Business: Meaning comes from personalizing the universal, but universals are really dull unless you can see them through someone's eyes. Here are five universals for every business: create shareholder value; the customer comes first; innovate or die; people are our greatest asset; continuous improvement. Restate one of these in terms that personalize it. For a CEO, one value could be to "create shareholder value to keep the stock price high enough that we can make another acquisition this year." For a sales executive, it could be "Continuous improvement keeps us in a position to give our customers the best value for the dollar." See if you can restate all five universal values in terms appropriate to your job.

Individual: At a personal level, the same universals also provide meaning. For you, they might be "I want my company to succeed so that I have the money to send Johnny to college" or "I was put on this Earth to serve other people." When you can articulate in personal terms what gives meaning to you, you'll have an easier time seeing what gives meaning to other people's lives. If you can bring this aesthetic sensibility and the artist within you to your work, you can do great things.

Another Way of Looking at Things

Picasso and Einstein both radically reshaped our sense of time, space, and light. They never met or seemed interested in each other's work, yet they shared a strikingly similar vision of our world. So much so that the comedian-actor-playwright Steve Martin wrote a play, *Picasso at the Lapin Agile*, about what they might have discussed had they actually met and talked in a bohemian Paris bistro in 1904.[1]

Art and science are two ways to understand our existence, our world, and our reality. They are distinct, complementary explorations of the same cosmos. They work two sides of the same street, but they too rarely draw from one another. Both introduce new visions and unfamiliar ideas that eventually change civilization. Both art and science have intermediaries whose job is to interpret their insights and show their applications in practical realms, such as health, education, politics, and business.

Science tells us how the world operates, and technology gives us practical applications of the insights. These make their way into the products and services of the economy. The path leading to economic activity is the flow from universe to science to technology to business. Engineers are the intermediaries helping to bring science to economy.

The arts, by contrast, tell us how people operate and what they can create and appreciate. This path leads from universe to arts to performance to social expression. Performers are the intermediaries helping to bring the arts to society.

Performers are to the arts what engineers are to science. Both are interpreters of revolutionary insights, one drawing on the internal space of imagination (gestures, tones, emotions), the other on the external space of investigation (observations, measurements, laws). Engineers and performers use different tools and methods and speak different languages, but their work is rooted in the same larger purpose: to decode and comprehend our world. The subjective, internal reality of the arts and the objective, external reality of the sciences are mirror interpretations of the same singular reality.

Business has drawn more readily from science than from art, but it could gain from seeing more common ground with art. If science and art can learn from each other, as with Picasso and Einstein and with Da Vinci and Pacioli, then business and art can, too.

Our purpose in writing *The Art of Business* has been to show how some of the basic constructs and models we use to view the world—economic and artistic—can complement one another. An artistic perspective, something that managers generally don't have as much experience with, can help produce great business as well as a perspective that is based in science and engineering.

You don't need to be an "artist" every day to tap into the artistic flow, and you don't need to dress up like one or even act like one. Just as artistic flow can influence your business, an artistic perspective inside you can be a critical part of every important thing you want to do. With it, you are already a sometimes artist. With it, you'll see how having an artistic sensibility benefits your business, your work, and your life.

NOTES

CHAPTER ONE: THE ARTISTIC FLOW OF BUSINESS

1. F. Scott Fitzgerald, *The Crack-Up* (New York: J. Laughlin, 1945).

2. C. P. Snow, *The Two Cultures* (Cambridge, Eng.: Cambridge University Press, 1959).

CHAPTER TWO: DUALITIES

1. Roger Fisher and William Ury, *Getting to Yes: Negotiating Agreement Without Giving In* (Boston: Houghton Mifflin, 1992).

CHAPTER THREE: THE ELEMENTS OF ARTISTIC FLOW

1. Mihaly Csikszentmihalyi, *Flow: The Psychology of Optimal Experience* (New York: Harper Collins Publishers, 1990).

2. Daniel Goleman, Annie McKee, and Richard E. Boyatzis, *Primal Leadership: Realizing the Power of Emotional Intelligence* (Boston: Harvard Business School Press, 2002).

3. Howard Gardner, *Frames of Mind: The Theory of Multiple Intelligences* (New York: Basic Books, 1983).

4. Ross King, *Brunelleschi's Dome: How a Renaissance Genius Reinvented Architecture* (New York: Walker & Company, 2000).

5. Viktor Frankl, *Man's Search for Meaning: An Introduction to Logotherapy* (Boston: Beacon Press, 1959), 154.

Notes

6. Tom Peters, *The Pursuit of WOW!* (New York: Vintage Books USA, 1994).

7. Jacques Duffourg, "Jean-Sébastien Bach, le Roi, danse," found on http://www.resmusica.com/imprimer.php3?art=188, July 3, 2002.

8. Robert Pirsig, *Zen and the Art of Motorcycle Maintenance: An Inquiry into Values* (New York: William Morrow and Company, 1974).

CHAPTER FOUR: ARTISTIC INPUTS IN BUSINESS

1. This story is recounted on a number of websites of notable quotations, including http://www.brainyquote.com/quotes/authors/howard_ikemoto.html.

2. Paul Ekman, E. Richard Sorenson, and Wallace V. Friesen, "Pan-Cultural Elements in Facial Displays of Emotions," *Science* 164, no. 3875 (1969): 86–88.

3. Daniel Goleman, *Emotional Intelligence: Why It Can Matter More Than IQ* (New York: Bantam Books, 1995).

4. Robert Kelley and Janet Caplan, "How Bell Labs Creates Star Performers," *Harvard Business Review*, July–August 1993, 128–39.

5. More information about Kimbell and her art can be found on her website, http://www.lucykimbell.com.

6. The Heisenberg Uncertainty Principle states that you can know where a subatomic particle is or where it's going, but not both at the same time; in measuring one you influence the other. The Hawthorne Effect is the tendency for a group's productivity to increase when it is being studied simply because of the additional attention it receives.

Notes

7. Interview on National Public Radio, *Talk of the Nation*, April 8, 2004.

8. T. P. Wright, "Learning Curve," *Journal of the Aeronautical Science* (February 1936), cited in Wikipedia, http://en.wikipedia .org/wiki/Experience_curve_effects.

9. This and many other quotes attributed to entertainer and humorist Will Rogers can be found at http://cmgworldwide.com/ historic/rogers/quotes5.htm.

10. Quoted in Peter L. Bernstein, *Against the Gods* (New York: John Wiley & Sons, 1996).

11. B. Joseph Pine II and James Gilmore, *The Experience Economy* (Boston: Harvard Business School Press, 1999).

12. Rakesh Khurana, *Searching for a Corporate Savior: The Irrational Quest for Charismatic CEOs* (Princeton, NJ: Princeton University Press, 2002).

CHAPTER FIVE: TELL YOUR STORY, WRITE YOUR POEM, SING YOUR SONG

1. Louis V. Gerstner, Jr., *Who Says Elephants Can't Dance?* (New York: Harper Business, 2002), 43.

2. Stephen Kinzer, "A Passion for Poetry (and Profits)," *The New York Times*, April 19, 2004.

3. Dana Gioia, *The Gods of Winter* (St. Paul, MN: Graywolf Press, 1991).

4. Dana Gioia, "Can Poetry Matter?" *The Atlantic Monthly*, May 1991, 94–106.

5. Mary Pinard, in interview with the authors, July 29, 2003.

Notes

6. Benson P. Shapiro, V. Kasturi Rangan, and John J. Sviokla, "Staple Yourself to an Order," *Harvard Business Review*, July–August 1992, 113–22.

CHAPTER SIX: ARTISTIC PROCESSES IN BUSINESS

1. Twyla Tharp, *The Creative Habit* (New York: Simon & Schuster, 2003).

2. Betty Edwards, *Drawing on the Artist Within* (New York: Simon & Schuster, 1986).

3. Mikko Nissinen, in interview with the authors, July 30, 2003.

4. Barbara Minto, *The Minto Pyramid Principle* (London: Minto International, 1996).

5. K. Anders Ericsson, R. T. Krampe, and C. Tesch-Romer, "The Role of Deliberate Practice in the Acquisition of Expert Performance," *Psychological Review* 100 (1993): 363–406.

6. Belle Linda Halpern and Kathy Lubar, *Leadership Presence* (New York: Gotham Books, 2003).

7. Gerald Clarke, "Two Lives, One Ambition," *Time*, April 2, 1990, 64.

8. "Face Value: Queen of the Online Flea Market," *Economist*, January 3, 2004.

CHAPTER SEVEN: FIND THE ARTISTIC IN EVERYTHING YOU DO

1. Peter Drucker, *The Practice of Management* (New York: Harper & Row, 1954), 39.

Notes

2. Arthur C. Clarke, *Profiles of the Future: An Inquiry into the Limits of the Possible*, rev. ed. (1962; repr., London: Orions Books, 2000).

3. Mitchell Resnick, "It's Not Just Information," *IBM Systems Journal* 39 (2000), found on http://www.research.ibm.com/journal/sj/393/part2/resnick.html.

4. Hiawatha Bray, "Study: File Downloads Don't Affect Sales of CDs," *The Boston Globe*, March 31, 2004.

CHAPTER EIGHT: ARTISTIC OUTPUTS IN BUSINESS

1. Alfred P. Sloan, Jr., *My Years with General Motors* (Garden City, NY: Doubleday Anchor, 1972), 316.

2. Ibid., 273.

3. Rich Thomaselli, "'What Happens Here, Stays Here' Becomes Cultural Phenomenon," *Advertising Age*, March 8, 2004.

4. John Sculley, *Odyssey: Pepsi to Apple, A Journey of Adventure, Ideas, and the Future* (New York: Harper & Row, 1987), 90.

5. Studs Terkel, *Working: People Talk About What They Do All Day and How They Feel About What They Do* (New York: Pantheon Books, 1974).

CHAPTER NINE: DO YOUR
CUSTOMERS SEND YOU ENERGY?

1. Francis Duffy, *The Changing Workplace* (London: Phaidon Press, 1992).

2. Bradford McKee, "What's Design Got to Do With It?" *The New York Times*, July 31, 2003.

Notes

3. Charna Halpern, Del Close, and Kim Johnson, *Truth in Comedy* (Colorado Springs, CO: Meriwether Publishing, 1994).

4. Dave Carpenter, "Funny Business," *St. Paul Pioneer Press*, July 19, 2004.

EXIT MUSIC

1. Steve Martin, *Picasso at the Lapin Agile* (New York: Samuel French, Inc., 1996).

ACKNOWLEDGMENTS

Good art, like good work, is never made in a vacuum. We are lucky to have had the support and advice of many gifted people. Three deserve particular mention. Without them, this book never would have been conceived, written, and published.

Marc Scorca, the president of Opera America, values the cross-pollenization between the worlds of art and business more than anyone else we know. He has looked to us to bring business thinking into the arts community, while we have been learning from him how a great leader works. Marc provided the inspiring spark that started us on this book, and he kept pushing, challenging, and supporting us for the next two years.

Rafe Sagalyn, our agent, showed us what it's like to really believe in your work. Even while telling us that the book wasn't ready for prime time, that we needed more time to immerse and simmer, he never gave up on us. Without him, we never would have found our audience.

Steve Piersanti, our editor and the president of Berrett-Koehler Publishers, is both a visionary and a remarkably subtle coach. While it's easy to see what's wrong with a manuscript and not that much harder to know what would be better, the art comes in getting writers to see how they can get from here to there on their own. Steve is an artist who makes Berrett-Koehler a work of art.

We benefited immeasurably from the contributions of the people who read earlier versions of the manuscript. The effort they in-

Acknowledgments

vested in sharpening our arguments and improving our prose was an undeserved gift. We especially want to thank Scott Borg, Joel Friedman, Lucy Kimbell, Jennifer Liss, Ann Sonz Matranga, Joe Pine, Crystal Reiss, and Jenny Williams for their many detailed suggestions. Also providing valuable input on the manuscript were Don Abraham, Ann Meier Baker, Mel Blake, Alain Dumont, Henry Fogel, Bill Gregor, Wolfgang Grulke, Roberto Panzarani, Gregory Peterson, Howard Schwartz, Andrea Snyder, and Diane Wondisford.

As we were getting started on this book, we interviewed several people from the arts world, the business world, and the academic world. We are particularly indebted to Jessica Davis, Janice Mancini Del Sesto, John Humphrey, Lewis Lloyd, Ed Nilsson, Mikko Nissinen, Anne Peretz, Mary Pinard, Peter Testa, and Valerie Wilder for having such an impact on our understanding of the economic and artistic flows.

Chris Meyer, formerly the director of the Center of Business Innovation and now the CEO of The Monitor Networks, is the matchmaker behind our partnership. He gave the two of us our first opportunity to work together, in 1998, when he and Stan had just published *Blur.* If anybody knows something about the artistic flow of business, it's Chris.

Finally, we want to thank our spouses, Barbara Davis and Leah McIntosh. As we were writing this book, they saw both too much and too little of us. To them go our apologies and our gratitude.

INDEX

Index

Index

Index

Index

Index

Index

Index

Index

Index

Index

Index

Index

ABOUT THE AUTHORS

STAN DAVIS is a highly respected commentator on business in the future. He is the author of twelve other books, including the best-sellers *Blur*, *2020 Vision*, and *Future Perfect*, as well as *It's Alive!* and *The Monster Under the Bed*. His creative thinking makes practical connections to new business opportunities, and his restive mind has led him into and out of many fields. With a doctorate in the social sciences and an honorary doctorate in the humanities, Stan spent twenty years as an academic, mainly on the faculty of the Harvard Business School. For the past two decades he has been active in re-search, writing, consulting, public speaking, seminars, training, and video. He is a Publications Board Advisor at the *New England Journal of Medicine*. Stan was a member of the Board of Directors of the Boston Ballet for sixteen years and of Jacob's Pillow Dance Center for six years, and he has served on the Board of Directors of Opera America, the trade association of 197 opera companies, for the past six years.

DAVID McINTOSH is a consultant, writer, and speaker who works with groups of executives to improve their leadership effectiveness. An expert in the field of executive development, he creates cus-tomized, high-impact programs for CEOs and their leadership teams. While working at the CGE&Y Center for Business Innova-tion, David created and led the CBI Network, a global community of innovators and thought leaders in fifteen countries. His 24-month

About the Authors

Future Scan was broadcast by internet to a live audience on six continents twice a year. He has also worked as a consultant at Mercer Management Consulting and as a real estate investment banker at Sonnenblick-Goldman Corp. He received his MBA and AB degrees from Harvard University. David has been a featured speaker for groups in North America, Europe, and Asia. His writing has appeared in publications including *Urban Land* and *Perspectives on Business Innovation*. He is on the Board of Directors of Opera America.